THE DUTCH
COOKBOOK

THE DUTCH
COOKBOOK

VAN DISHOECK

© 1988 this edition by Unieboek b.v., P.O. Box 97, 3990
DB Houten
Cover design: Julie Bergen
Photography: Editors Holland
Translation: Jan Morgan
Original title: De echte Nederlandse keuken
NUGI 421
ISBN 90 269 3348 7

Contents

Introduction

Dutch food is, on the whole, substantial and straightforward. The national cuisine of Holland has, in this respect, been strongly influenced by the constant struggle to reclaim land from the sea in order to turn it into rich farming land. The long wet and windy winters have also had an effect on eating patterns in The Netherlands – people needed food rich in fat as protection against the elements. Add to this the fact that a large percentage of the population used to be either involved in farming the land or fishing the coastal waters and one can easily justify a high-calorie diet.

Since the war automation has become the order of the day – even jobs on farms are far more sedentary than they used to be and vast meals are a thing of the past. Nutritionalists advise low-fat and low-salt diets to help to prevent heart disease and a wide range of low-fat dairy products (milk being a staple ingredient in the Dutch diet) is widely available. Cattle are also being bred to produce leaner meat and vegetable oils and polyunsaturated margarines have long replaced bacon fat and butter, which used to have pride of place in the Dutch kitchen. The Dutch still enjoy the much-loved winter soups and casseroles, which used to be served up with an extra ladle of melted bacon fat to keep out the cold and this book contains recipes for a wide variety of traditional and also for less well-known Dutch dishes. The arrival of new and imported vegetables (peppers, courgettes, broccoli etc.) has broadened the culinary scope of today's housewife, but many still turn to favourite recipes passed down from mother to daughter and then adapt them to suit their own families' needs, using modern cooking methods.

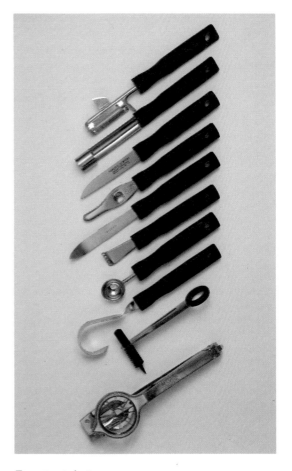

From top to bottom:
1. potato peeler
2. apple corer
3. paring knife
4. citrus peeler
5. grapefruit knife
6. citrus zester
7. melon ball cutter
8. butter curler
9. vegetable curler
10. radish cutter

All recipes are for 4 people unless otherwise stated.

Kitchen equipment and measurements

Professional kitchens in restaurants and hotels nearly always have an array of well cared for, high quality equipment and it is well worth while investing in good kitchen equipment in your own home which will remain efficient even after years of service.

Everything is relative, however, and, for example, it is not necessary to have a complete set of copper pans in order to be able to cook well. It is, however, a fact that egg whites beaten in a copper bowl will retain their volume for much longer than egg whites beaten in an earthenware bowl due to the chemical reaction between the egg white and the copper. The choice between aluminium, stainless steel, cast iron, enamel and copper kitchenware remains a personal choice and depends of course on the extent of your household budget.

High prices do not always ensure good quality. One of the best places to buy good kitchenware is either at a well known and reliable hardware store or at a shop dealing in hotel and restaurant ware. Take your families' needs into consideration – if you prepare a lot of deep fried food then it is worthwhile investing in a deep fryer – a fish kettle is essential for those who enjoy plenty of fresh fish.

The following list of kitchen equipment can be used as a guide for those setting up a new home or kitchen.

– set of 3 pans with lids
– 1 small and 1 large frying pan
– deep fryer
– 2 small milk pans
– 1 or 2 flameproof casseroles
– 1 bread board and several small chopping boards
– 1 sharp breadknife
– 1 knife sharpener
– 1 pair of kitchen scissors
– 1 paring knife
– 1 potato peeler
– 1 set of chopping knives
– 1 palette knife
– 1 carving knife
– 1 applecorer
– 1 egg slicer
– 1 canelling knife
– 1 tomato cutter

– 1 asparagus peeler
– 1 all purpose grater
– 1 butter curler
– set of pastry cutters
– several wire whisks
– several wooden spoons
– 1 colander
– pair of scales
– 1 draining spoon
– several ladles
– 1 ice scoop
– set of salad servers
– 1 anti-splash pan cover
– 1 set of sieves
– 1 or more rechauds

Make sure that all kitchen equipment is kept scrupulously clean, especially wooden chopping boards – these are best cleaned with soap and plenty of hot water.

Measurements

The required weight or volume of the ingredients is given in grams. Imperial (British) and American equivalents follow in that order.

American cup measurements are not as exact as imperial and metric measurements. A cup of flour for example could be lightly or heavily packed and this can influence the metric or imperial equivalent by as much as 50 g (2 oz). The American equivalents given here are based on level cupfuls of the ingredient mentioned.

Always add liquids slowly and add a little extra flour or liquid to doughs and pastries should they be either too sticky or too dry. If in doubt, measure dry ingredients in ounces – this will give a more accurate result. Remember that 1 imperial pint is equivalent to 20 fl oz and that 1 American pint is equivalent to only 16 fl oz.

Stuffed eggs

(Gevulde eieren)

serves 4-8

8 eggs
100 g (4 oz) (½ cup) soft butter
2 tbs (1½ tbs) (1½ tbs) cream
2 tsp (1½ tsp) (1½ tsp) finely grated cheese
1 tsp (½ tsp) (½ tsp) made mustard
1 tbs (½ tbs) (½ tbs) tomato paste
1 tbs (½ tbs) (½ tbs) finely chopped parsley
salt, freshly ground pepper
4 tbs (3 tbs) (3 tbs) finely chopped curly endive

1. Hardboil the eggs, plunge them into cold water and remove the shells. Cut them in half lengthwise, remove the yolks and rub these through a fine sieve. Beat in the butter and the cream with a hand mixer until the mixture is light and fluffy.
2. Flavour one half of the butter mixture with the grated cheese and mustard and the other half with the tomato paste. Work the chopped parsley into the cheese mixture and season both with salt and pepper.
3. Spoon the cheese filling into a piping bag with a large fluted nozzle and pipe it into half of the egg whites. Fill the rest with the piped tomato filling.
4. Arrange the stuffed eggs on an attractive plate and garnish with the finely chopped curly endive.

Stuffed eggs with different fillings – always popular as a cold starter.

Prawn cocktail

(Garnalencocktail)

200 g (8 oz) (8 ounces) prawns
2-3 dl (7-10 fl oz) (1-1¼ cups) cocktail sauce
(see p. 27)
2 radishes
salt
freshly ground black pepper
1 tomato
a few sprigs parsley
1 well scrubbed lemon or lime

1. Pick over the prawns and discard any discoloured ones, rinse quickly with cold running water and drain well.
Meanwhile, prepare the cocktail sauce.
2. Wash the radishes, slice them as thinly as possible and season with a little salt and pepper.
3. Wash the tomato and cut into wedges.
4. Wash a few attractive sprigs of parsley and dry them with kitchen paper.
5. Cut two neat slices of lemon or lime and cut each slice in half.
6. Spoon the prawns into 4 cocktail glasses and cover with cocktail sauce.
7. Garnish each portion with a few slices of radish, a wedge of tomato and a sprig of parsley. Make a small cut in the peel at the end of each slice of lemon and press one onto the rim of each glass as shown in the photograph.

Note:
The Dutch favour the small salty prawns found in the North Sea, but any can be used – other Europeans prefer the larger, slightly sweet Norwegian prawn.

Cheese balls

(Kaasballetjes)

makes approx. 40 cheese balls

100 g (4 oz) (½ cup) soft butter
100 g (4 oz) (1⅓ cups) grated sharp cheese

Prawn cocktail with a delicious sauce.

cayenne pepper
½ tsp (¼ tsp) (¼ tsp) curry powder
2 tbs (1½ tbs) (1½ tbs) poppy or sesame seeds

1. Beat the butter and the grated cheese in a small deep bowl and season with a pinch of cayenne pepper and the curry powder.
2. Shape the mixture with cool hands into small balls approximately 2 cm (¾ inch) in diameter and roll them in the poppy or sesame seeds. Keep the hands cool by rinsing them occasionally with cold water. Dry well.
3. Arrange the cheese balls on a plate, cover with plastic film and chill for at least 30 minutes before serving.

Savoury tartlets

(Gevulde deegbakjes)

Cocktail snack

ready made pastry cases
2 dl (7 fl oz) (¾ cup) cocktail sauce (see p. 27)
made mustard
tomato ketchup
prawns or crab
cooked chicken breast
leftover cold meat
finely chopped parsley or chives
fresh or dried herbs and spices
grated horseradish (from a jar)
sliced hard boiled egg
grated cheese
finely chopped spring onions or shallots
finely chopped leek
thick fresh cream or sour cream

Use individual ready made pastry cases which are available in most supermarkets to make these tasty cocktail snacks. Several delicious fillings can be made using cocktail sauce, thick cream or sour cream as a base. Leftover meat, fish, poultry and vegetables can be combined with fresh fruit and your own favourite herbs and spices to make quick, easy fillings. Many types of English, American and continental cheeses can also be either grated or chopped fine, mixed with cream or yoghurt and flavoured with mustard or pickles to make interesting savoury fillings.

Tip:
The fillings can all be prepared in advance and then kept in the refrigerator. Fill the pastry cases just before serving to ensure that the pastry remains crisp.

Hussar's salad

(Huzarensalade)

350 g (12 oz) (12 ounces) cold meat, ham or sausage
4 medium boiled potatoes
2-3 eggs
2 sharp eating apples
4 large gherkins or sweet pickles
1 boiled beetroot
12 cocktail onions
5 tbs (4 tbs) (4 tbs) mayonnaise (see p. 26)
1 tsp (½ tsp) (½ tsp) made mustard
1 tsp (½ tsp) (½ tsp) cider vinegar
sugar to taste
salt
freshly ground pepper
a few lettuce leaves
a little finely chopped parsley or chives

1. Chop the cold meat, ham or sausage.
2. Cut the potatoes into cubes (1-2 cm) (½-¾ inch).
3. Shell the eggs and chop finely.
4. Peel the apples, remove the cores and cut into small cubes.
5. Finely chop the gherkins or sweet pickles, peel and chop the beetroot and put all the prepared ingredients into a large mixing bowl. Add the cocktail onions.
6. Mix the mayonnaise with the mustard and cider vinegar, sugar, salt and pepper to taste in a bowl.
7. Spoon the sauce carefully through the salad ingredients. Wash and dry the lettuce leaves (chop iceberg lettuce) and arrange them on a shallow dish. Pile the salad onto the bed of lettuce.
8. Garnish with chopped parsley or chives and serve with brown or white toast.

Note:
The name 'Hussar's salad' originates from the time when the hussars were stationed in small towns throughout Holland. As the food at the barracks was pretty dreadful, it was very important for the young soldiers to find a girlfriend who was also a kitchen maid. The hussars would steal out in the evening and charm the girls into making tasty salads from the leftover kitchen scraps. This became known as the 'Hussar's Salad'.

Potato salad

(Aardappelsalade)

approx. 500 g (1 lb) (1 pound) firm boiled potatoes
2-3 hard boiled eggs
1 medium onion
1 small leek
¾ dl (3 fl oz) (⅓ cup) corn or sunflower oil
¼ dl (2 tbs) (2 tbs) herb vinegar
1 tsp (½ tsp) (½ tsp) French mustard
1 tsp (½ tsp) (½ tsp) sugar
2 tbs (½ tbs) (½ tbs) finely chopped parsley
salt
½ tsp (¼ tsp) (¼ tsp) freshly ground black pepper
pinch ground paprika
a few lettuce leaves

1. Slice the potatoes fairly thickly (1 cm) (½ inch) or cut into cubes (1½ cm) (¾ inch) and put them into a large bowl.
2. Shell the eggs and slice thinly.
3. Peel and finely chop the onion. Clean and finely chop the leek and mix it with the potatoes.
4. Mix the oil, vinegar, mustard, sugar, parsley and chopped onion in a small bowl and season with salt, pepper and a pinch of ground paprika.
5. Pour the dressing over the potato mixture and mix well, taking care not to break up the potatoes.
6. Wash and dry the lettuce leaves and arrange them on a shallow plate. Spoon the potato salad onto the bed of lettuce and garnish with the sliced egg.

Dutch herring salad

(Haringsalade)

4 salted herrings
2 medium boiled potatoes
1 onion
1 firm apple
2 large gherkins or sweet pickles
1 cooked beetroot
4 tbs (3 tbs) (3 tbs) mayonnaise (see p. 26)
1 tsp (½ tsp) (½ tsp) made mustard
sugar to taste

salt
freshly ground pepper
alfalfa or bean sprouts
parsley

1. Split the salted herrings, remove the backbones and the tails and put the fillets on a flat plate.
2. Cut the potatoes into cubes (1 cm) (½ inch) and put them into a large mixing bowl. Peel and finely chop the onion; peel, core and chop the apple; chop the gherkins or pickles and the beetroot and add to the cubed potatoes.
3. Toss the salad ingredients, taking care not to break up the potatoes.
4. Mix the mayonnaise with the mustard, sugar, salt and pepper to taste in a small bowl.
5. Spoon the sauce carefully through the potato salad and spread a little over each herring fillet. Roll them up and secure with cocktail sticks.
6. Serve the herring on a bed of cleaned alfalfa or bean sprouts and garnish with finely chopped parsley if wished.

Meat scallops

(Vleesschelpjes)

250 g (8 oz) (8 ounces) cold beef, pork or veal
1 medium onion or 3 shallots
1 small leek
35 g (1½ oz) (3 tbs) butter
30 g (1 oz) (3 tbs) flour
1 dl (3½ fl oz) (⅓ cup) milk
1 dl (3½ fl oz) (⅓ cup) meat stock
1 tbs (½ tbs) (½ tbs) finely chopped parsley
salt
freshly ground pepper
ground nutmeg
4 large scallop shells
2 tbs (1½ tbs) (1½ tbs) dried breadcrumbs
butter

1. Finely chop the meat.
2. Peel and finely chop the onion or shallots. Clean the leek thoroughly, halve lengthwise and chop finely. Preheat the oven to 200 °C (400 °F).
3. Melt the butter in a heavy based pan and sauté

the onion and leek for a few minutes until soft.

4. Blend the sifted flour into the butter and cook for 2-3 minutes over a low heat, stirring continuously with a wooden spoon.

5. Gradually add the milk and stock, allowing the sauce to thicken and boil between each addition. When all the liquid has been added, bring to the boil and simmer gently for about 5 minutes to make a smooth sauce.

6. Stir the chopped meat, a little chopped parsley and salt, pepper and nutmeg to taste into the sauce and mix well.

7. Turn the ragout into 4 lightly greased scallop shells, sprinkle with breadcrumbs and dot with butter. Bake for 10-15 minutes or until the tops are golden brown.

Prawn scallops

(Garnalenschelpjes)

250 g (8 oz) (8 ounces) small prawns
1 small onion or 2 shallots, 1 small leek
35 g (1½ oz) (3 tbs) butter
30 g (1 oz) (3 tbs) flour
1 dl (3½ fl oz) (⅓ cup) milk
1 dl (3½ fl oz) (⅓ cup) fish stock
1 tbs (½ tbs) (½ tbs) finely chopped dill or chives
salt, freshly ground pepper, nutmeg
4 large scallop shells
2 tbs (1½ tbs) (1½ tbs) grated sharp cheese
4 slices fresh white toast

1. Pick over the prawns and remove any discoloured ones.

2. Prepare the sauce as described in the previous recipe (points 2-5 incl).

3. Stir the prawns into the sauce and season with chopped dill, salt, pepper and nutmeg to taste. Warm the prawns through in the sauce, but do not overcook, otherwise they will become tough.

4. Spoon the prawn mixture into the scallop shells and sprinkle with grated cheese.

5. Place the prawn scallops on the top shelf of a preheated oven (200 °C) (400 °F) and bake for 10-12 minutes or until the tops are golden brown. Serve immediately with fresh white toast.

Kidneys on fried bread

(Nierbroodjes)

1 calf's kidney, approx. 275 g (10 oz) (10 ounces)
salt
1 medium onion
30 g (1 oz) (2 tbs) butter
½ large carrot
2 dl (7 fl oz) (¾ cup) kidney stock
½ dl (2 fl oz) (¼ cup) milk
30 g (1 oz) (3 tbs) flour
freshly ground pepper, ground nutmeg
1 tbs (½ tbs) (½ tbs) finely chopped celery leaves
a few drops lemon juice
4-6 slices bread, without crusts
butter, for frying the bread
2 tbs (1 tbs) (1 tbs) finely chopped parsley

1. Soak the kidney for a few hours in several changes of cold water. Blanch it for 4 minutes in boiling water, drain and rinse well.

2. Put the blanched kidney in a pan, cover with water, add a little salt, bring to the boil and simmer gently for about 30 minutes. Drain and reserve 2 dl (7 fl oz) (¾ cup) of the liquid for the sauce.

3. Peel and finely chop the onion. Melt the butter in a heavy based saucepan and sauté the onion in the hot butter.

4. Peel and finely chop the carrot, add it to the onion and fry gently for a few minutes.

5. Mix the kidney stock with the milk and blend 3 tablespoons of the liquid with the flour. Pour the stock and milk over the sautéed onion and carrot and add the flour mixture, stirring continuously. Bring the sauce to the boil, still stirring and cook until smooth and thick.

6. Season the sauce with pepper, nutmeg, salt, chopped celery leaves and lemon juice.

7. Finely chop the kidney with a sharp knife or in a food processor and stir it into the hot sauce. Keep warm whilst preparing the fried bread.

8. Cut the slices of bread in half and fry them golden brown in hot butter. Arrange them on a warm flat dish and spoon a little of the hot kidney mixture over each one.

9. Garnish with finely chopped parsley and serve piping hot.

Veal croquettes

(Kalfskroketten)

approx. 200 g (8 oz) (8 ounces) cold veal
1 medium onion
100 g (4 oz) (4 ounces) boiled potatoes
30 g (1 oz) (2 tbs) butter
30 g (1 oz) (3 tbs) flour
2 dl (7 fl oz) (¾ cup) veal stock
2 tbs (2 tbs) (2 tbs) finely chopped parsley
salt, pepper, ground nutmeg
dried breadcrumbs
2 egg whites
oil or fat for deep frying

1. Finely chop the cold veal. Peel and chop the onion. Mash the boiled potatoes.
2. Heat the butter in a heavy based pan and sauté the onion until soft. Blend in the flour and cook for 2-3 minutes over a low heat, stirring continuously with a wooden spoon. Gradually add the veal stock, allowing the sauce to thicken and boil between each addition. When all the stock has been added, bring to the boil and simmer gently for about 5 minutes to make a smooth sauce.
3. Stir the veal and potatoes into the sauce, mix well and add the parsley, salt, pepper and nutmeg.
4. The croquette mixture should be firm, but not dry. Add a little extra stock or milk if necessary.
5. Spread the mixture onto a wet plate and leave until cool. Shape into croquettes or patties and coat firstly with breadcrumbs, then with beaten egg white and finally with another layer of breadcrumbs.
6. Heat the fat or oil in a chip pan or deep fryer with basket and fry the croquettes, a few at a time, until golden brown. Remove from the pan and drain on kitchen paper. Serve piping hot on warm plates and garnish with lettuce if wished.

Variation:
Shape the mixture into small balls and coat with egg and breadcrumbs. Deep fry until golden brown and drain on kitchen paper. Pierce each one with a cocktail stick and serve piping hot with sharp mustard. These delicious cocktail snacks are known as 'bitterballen' in Holland and are available in most bars, cafes and restaurants.

Cheese puffs

(Kaassoesjes)

makes approx. 48 small puffs

50 g (2 oz) (4 tbs) butter
salt
50 g (2 oz) (6 tbs) flour
2 eggs

for the filling:
200 g (8 oz) (2 ⅔ cup) grated sharp cheese
200 g (8 oz) (1 cup) soft butter
freshly ground pepper

1. Bring 1 dl (3½ dl oz) (⅓ cup) water to the boil in a small heavy based pan, add the butter and salt to taste. Tip the flour into the boiling water and stir until the mixture forms a ball which easily comes away from the sides of the pan.
2. Remove the pan from the heat and beat in the eggs, one by one.
3. Continue beating until the mixture is glossy and firm but pliable. Preheat the oven to 200 °C (400 °F).
4. Pile the mixture into a piping bag fitted with a fairly wide plain nozzle and pipe small heaps, about the size of a walnut, onto a greased baking sheet. Allow space between the puffs for the mixture to spread (approx. 5 cm or 2 inches).
5. Place the baking sheet in the centre of the oven and bake the puffs for approximately 25 minutes or until they are light golden brown and well risen. Cool on a wire cooling tray.
6. Split the puffs open with the point of a sharp knife and fill with creamy cheese butter. Recipe below.

Filling:
1. Beat the grated cheese into the softened butter and season with pepper and maybe with a little curry powder or ground paprika.
2. Fill the puffs with this mixture and serve at once or cover and refrigerate until required.

Fishcakes

(Viskoekjes)

makes approx. 15 fishcakes

approx. 500 g (1 lb) (1 pound) cooked fish (cod, haddock etc.)
2 slices white bread
2 dl (7 fl oz) (¾ cup) milk
1-2 eggs
1 onion
1 small leek
salt
freshly ground pepper
ground nutmeg
2 tbs (1½ tbs) (1½ tbs) finely chopped parsley
4 tbs (3 tbs) (3 tbs) dried breadcrumbs or flour
60 g (2 oz) (4 tbs) butter

1. Mash the fish with a fork or chop it in the food processor and transfer to a mixing bowl.
2. Remove the crusts from the bread and soak it in the milk for about 5 minutes. Squeeze it dry and stir into the mashed fish.
3. Lightly beat the eggs, peel and chop the onion and clean and chop the leek. Stir them all into the fish mixture and season with salt, pepper, nutmeg to taste and the chopped parsley.
4. Knead the mixture to a firm dough, adding a little flour or more soaked bread if necessary.
5. Shape into patties, approximately 7 cm (3 inches) across or into croquettes.
6. Coat the fishcakes with dried breadcrumbs and shallow fry, a few at a time, until golden brown in the hot butter. Serve piping hot.

Tip:
Use mashed potato or half bread, half potato as a base for the fish cakes, instead of the soaked bread. Fish cakes can also be deep fried – coat them with beaten egg and crumbs to prevent them from splitting open in the hot fat. Deep fried food has more calories than shallow fried food.

Cheese patties

(Kaaskoekjes)

makes approx. 20 patties

30 g (1 oz) (2 tbs) butter
30 g (1 oz) (3 tbs) flour
2 dl (7 fl oz) (¾ cup) milk
approx. 175 g (6 oz) (2½ cups) grated mature cheese
salt
freshly ground pepper
dried breadcrumbs or flour
1 egg
fat or oil for deep frying

1. Melt the butter in a heavy based pan, blend in the flour and cook for 2-3 minutes over low heat, stirring continuously with a wooden spoon.
2. Gradually add the milk, allowing the sauce to thicken and boil between each addition. When all the milk has been added, bring to the boil and simmer gently for about 5 minutes to make a smooth sauce.
3. Remove the pan from the heat and gradually stir in the grated cheese – heat through if necessary until the cheese has melted, but do not bring back to the boil.
4. Season with salt, pepper and possibly with a little ground paprika or curry powder and turn the mixture onto a wet plate or marble slab. Leave until cold.
5. Shape into round or square patties and coat with breadcrumbs or flour. Beat the egg on a plate and coat the patties with beaten egg and then with more breadcrumbs or flour.
6. Deep fry, a few at a time, in hot fat or oil until golden brown, drain on kitchen paper and serve piping hot.

Soups

Fish stock

(Visbouillon)

300 g (10 oz) (10 ounces) fish heads and bones
200 g (8 oz) (8 ounces) haddock or cod
1 medium onion
1 large carrot
1 leek
piece fennel bulb
3 sprigs parsley
1 finely chopped stick celery
the rind of 1 lemon
1 tsp (½ tsp) (½ tsp) white peppercorns
pinch thyme
salt

1. Put the cleaned fish heads and bones, the cod or haddock and 1½ (2¾ pts) (6 cups) water into a large pan and bring slowly to the boil.
2. Peel and roughly chop the onion and the carrot. Clean and roughly chop the leek and the fennel. Wash the parsley.
3. Add the prepared vegetables and herbs to the pan, together with the lemon rind (well scrubbed), peppercorns, thyme and salt to taste.
4. Reduce the heat once the stock has come to the boil, cover the pan and simmer very gently for 30-40 minutes.
9. Strain the stock through a fine sieve or a piece of muslin and use as required.

Tip:
A good way of storing leftover meat, chicken, fish or vegetable stock is to reduce it over a fierce heat and then freeze it in small containers (ice cube trays for example). Use the concentrated stock to flavour soups and sauces.

Beef stock

(Runderbouillon)

500 g (1 lb) (1 pound) shin of beef
2 marrow bones
1 medium onion
1 leek
1 large carrot
3 sprigs parsley
1 stick celery, roughly chopped
1 bay leaf
small piece of mace
1 tsp (½ tsp) (½ tsp) peppercorns
pinch thyme
pinch basil
salt

1. Put the shin of beef, marrow bones and 1½ l (2¾ pts) (6 cups) water into a large pan and bring slowly to the boil.
2. Peel and quarter the onion; wash and roughly chop the leek, peel and roughly chop the carrot, wash the parsley.
3. Add the prepared vegetables and herbs to the pan, together with the bay leaf, mace, roughly crushed peppercorns, thyme, basil and salt to taste.
4. Reduce the heat as soon as the stock has come to the boil, skim the surface and simmer very gently for 4 hours. Strain through a fine sieve or a piece of muslin and serve as consommé, or use as a base for sauces and ragouts etc.

Variation:
Use pig's trotters or a mixture of pork and veal meat and bones instead of beef. Simmer the stock no longer than 1-1/2 hours, strain through a fine sieve or a piece of muslin and use as a base for clear soup etc.

Vegetable stock

(Groentebouillon)

2 medium onions
2 leeks
1 large carrot
100 g (4 oz) (4 ounces) cauliflower
100 g (4 oz) (4 ounces) white cabbage
3 sprigs parsley
1 stick celery, roughly chopped
small piece of mace
1 bay leaf
1 tsp (½ tsp) (½ tsp) peppercorns
salt

1. Bring 1½ l (2¾ pts) (6 cups) water slowly to the boil in a large pan.
2. Peel and thickly slice the onions; wash and roughly chop the leeks, peel and roughly chop the carrot.
3. Wash the cauliflower and break into flowerets, wash and finely chop the cabbage, rinse the parsley.
4. Add the prepared vegetables and herbs to the pan of water, together with the mace, bay leaf, roughly crushed peppercorns and salt to taste.
5. Reduce the heat as soon as the water has come to the boil, cover and simmer very gently for approximately 1 hour. Strain the stock through a fine sieve or muslin and use as required.

Tip:
A quicker way to prepare a tasty vegetable stock is to dissolve vegetable stock cubes in the water before adding the chopped vegetables and herbs. Simmer gently for 30 minutes and add salt to taste. Commercially prepared stock cubes usually have salt added, so very little extra will be required. Follow the directions on the packet as to the number of cubes required for the above amount of water.

Chicken stock

(Kippebouillon)

600-700 g (1-1½ lbs) (1-1½ pounds) chicken bones and scraps (necks, wingtips etc.)
1 large onion
2 leeks
1 large carrot
3 sprigs parsley
1 stick celery, roughly chopped
small piece of mace
1 bay leaf
rind of 1 lemon (well scrubbed)
salt
1 tsp (½ tsp) (½ tsp) white peppercorns

1. Bring 1½ l (2¾ pts) (6 cups) water to the boil in a large saucepan. Rinse the chicken scraps with cold water and add them to the pan.
2. Peel and roughly chop the onion; wash and roughly chop the leeks, peel and roughly chop the carrot, wash the parsley.
3. Add the prepared vegetables and herbs to the pan, together with the mace, bay leaf, lemon rind, salt and roughly crushed peppercorns.
4. Reduce the heat as soon as the stock comes to the boil, skim the surface, cover the pan and simmer very gently for 2½ hours. Strain the stock through a fine sieve or muslin and use as required.

Noodle soup with meatballs

(Vermicellisoep)

1 l (1¾ pts) (4 cups) meat stock (see p. 16)
40 g fine noodles (vermicelli)
75 g (3 oz) (3 ounces) minced veal
½ slice white bread
1 tbs (½ tbs) (½ tbs) lightly beaten egg
1 tbs (½ tbs) (½ tbs) cream
freshly ground pepper
salt
ground nutmeg
ground mace
grated cheese

1. Bring the stock to the boil and add the noodles as the stock reaches boiling point.
2. Mix the minced veal with the crumbled bread (crusts removed), a little beaten egg and a dash of cream and season to taste with pepper, salt, nutmeg and mace.
3. Shape the seasoned mince into small marble sized balls and poach them for 15 minutes in the stock.
4. Serve the soup with grated cheese and breadsticks or fresh croutons.

Variations:
Use 30 g (1 oz) (1 ounce) rice instead of fine noodles and cook for 25 minutes or until the rice is tender. Add a little finely chopped spring onion and carrot for extra flavour.

Mushroom soup

(Champignonsoep)

150 g (6 oz) (3 cups) button mushrooms
1 onion
1 leek
40 g (1½ oz) (3 tbs) butter
40 g (1½ oz) (4 tbs) flour
1 l (1¾ pts) (4 cups) chicken or vegetable stock (see p. 17)
½ dl (2 fl oz) (¼ cup) lightly soured cream
salt

freshly ground black pepper
grated nutmeg

1. Wipe the mushrooms – do not soak in water – and slice them thinly.
2. Peel and chop the onion, wash and thinly slice the leek.
3. Melt the butter in a heavy based pan and sauté the onion, leek and sliced mushrooms until soft. Stir in the flour and gradually add the (warm) stock, stirring all the time.
4. Cook gently until the soup has thickened slightly, remove the pan from the heat and stir in the soured cream.
5. Season with salt, pepper and a little nutmeg to taste.

Curry soup

(Kerriesoep)

1 l (1¾ pts) (4 cups) chicken or beef stock (see p. 17 or 16)
2½ tbs (2 tbs) (2 tbs) rice
1 tbs (½ tbs) (½ tbs) flour
1½ tbs (1 tbs) (1 tbs) mild curry powder
1 dl (3½ fl oz) (⅓ cup) single cream
salt
freshly ground black pepper
pinch ground paprika

1. Bring the stock to the boil in a large heavy based pan, add the rice and simmer gently for about 30 minutes or until the rice is cooked.
2. Blend the flour and curry powder with the cream and add to soup, stirring continuously. Simmer gently for about 4 minutes or until the soup has thickened slightly.
3. Season to taste with salt, pepper and paprika.

Variation:
Poach a few small meatballs in the soup (see recipe for Noodle soup on this page) or garnish with strips of omelette. A dash of sherry or white wine will add extra flavour.

Asparagus soup

(Aspergesoep)

approx. 600 g (1¼ lb) (1¼ pounds) fresh asparagus
8 dl (1½ pts) (3 cups) vegetable stock
2 dl (7 fl oz) (¾ cup) white wine
salt, freshly ground pepper
35 g (1½ oz) (3 tbs) butter
35 g (1½ oz) (4 tbs) flour
grated nutmeg
1 dl (3½ fl oz) (⅓ cup) single cream
finely chopped parsley

1. Scrape the asparagus and remove any fibrous pieces. Cut into pieces approximately 3 cm (1¼ inches) long.

2. Bring the stock to the boil and add the asparagus, wine, salt and pepper to taste. Reduce the heat and simmer gently for 20 minutes or until the asparagus is tender.

3. Strain the soup and keep the asparagus warm. Reserve the stock for the soup.

4. Melt the butter in a large heavy based pan and stir in the flour. Cook gently, stirring continuously for 2-3 minutes.

5. Stir in the stock, little by little and simmer until the soup has thickened slightly.

6. Add the asparagus and season with a little nutmeg. Remove the pan from the heat and stir in the cream.

7. Ladle into warm soup plates and garnish with a little chopped parsley.

Asparagus soup – for that special occasion.

Cream of tomato soup

(Gebonden tomatensoep)

750 g (1½ lb) (1½ pounds) ripe tomatoes
2 medium onions
1 leek
1 carrot
40 g (1½ oz) (3 tbs) butter
4 sprigs parsley
1 l (1¾ pts) (4 cups) meat or vegetable stock
pinch thyme
pinch ground mace
5 peppercorns
1 bay leaf
30 g (1 oz) (3 tbs) flour
1 dl (3½ fl oz) (⅓ cup) single cream
finely chopped parsley

1. Cut the tomatoes into small pieces. Peel and chop the onions, wash and thinly slice the leek and peel and chop the carrot.
2. Melt the butter in a large heavy based pan and sauté the onions and leek until soft.
3. Add the carrot, tomatoes and parsley and stew gently for about 5 minutes, stirring occasionally.
4. Meanwhile, heat the stock and stir it into the stewed vegetables, together with the thyme, mace, lightly crushed peppercorns and bay leaf, bring to the boil and simmer gently for 15-20 minutes over a low heat.
5. Strain the soup into a large pan. Blend the flour with a few spoonfuls of soup and use this to thicken the soup. Season with salt and pepper to taste.
6. Remove the pan from the heat and stir in the cream. Garnish with a little chopped parsley.

Variation:
Vary the basic soup by adding sautéed sliced mushrooms, finely sliced celery, small meatballs (see recipe for Noodle soup with meatballs on p. 18), grated cheese or a little chopped fennel.

Tip:
Serve the soup for lunch with breadsticks, warm French bread or fresh white toast (crusts removed) and a seasonal or potato salad.

Oxtail soup

(Ossestaartsoep)

1 oxtail
2 onions
1 large carrot
2 tomatoes
30 g (1 oz) (2 tbs) butter
2 tbs (1½ tbs) (1½ tbs) finely chopped parsley
1 stalk celery, finely chopped.
2 bay leaves
5 peppercorns
pinch thyme
salt
2 tbs (1½ tbs) (1½ tbs) flour
2 tbs (1 tbs) (1 tbs) Madeira or port

1. Chop the oxtail into small pieces approximately 5 cm (2 inches) long. Peel and chop the onions, peel and slice the carrot.
2. Wash and chop the tomatoes.
3. Heat the butter in a large heavy based pan and brown the pieces of oxtail and chopped onions in the hot butter. Add the carrot and tomatoes and sauté until soft. Stir in the finely chopped parsley and the celery and cook for another couple of minutes.
4. Add 1½ l (2¾ pts) (6 cups) water and bring to the boil. Stir in the bay leaves, lightly crushed peppercorns, thyme and salt to taste, cover the pan and simmer gently for approximately 3½ hours.
5. Strain the soup. Blend the flour with a little cold water and use this to thicken the soup. Remove the meat from the oxtail, cut it into small pieces and return to the soup.
6. Madeira or port to taste.

Mussel soup

(Mosselsoep)

1 kg (2 lb) (2 pounds) mussels, with shell
350 g (12 oz) (12 ounces) chopped fresh vegetables,
e.g. onion, leek, carrot, celery, parsley etc.
200 g (8 oz) (8 ounces) mashed potatoes
2 tbs (1½) (1½) finely chopped parsley or chives
1 tbs (½ tbs) (½ tbs) finely chopped dill
salt
freshly ground pepper

1. Scrub the mussels in running water and remove
any which are already open or which feel unusually
heavy. Trim away the beards.
2. Put the chopped vegetables into a large heavy
based pan, add a little water and arrange the
cleaned mussels on top. Bring the water to the boil,
cover the pan and cook for approximately 10 minutes or until all the shells are open.
3. Strain off the cooking liquid and reserve for the
soup. Discard any mussels which have remained
closed, remove the rest from their shells and put
them into a pan with the strained cooking liquid.
4. Make the liquid up to 1 l (1¾ pts) (4 cups) with
cold water, bring to the boil and use the mashed
potato to thicken the soup slightly.
5. Add the chopped parsley and dill and season to
taste with salt and pepper. Serve piping hot with
fresh toast or warm French bread.

Mussel and vegetable soup

(Zeeuwse mosselsoep)

A recipe from the southern Dutch province of Zee-
land where the mussels are cultivated in the shallow
waters of the Schelde. The mussel season begins in
late July and goes through to February or March.
The best mussels are those caught between August
and December – after that the quality is noticeably
poorer.

1 kg (2 lb) (2 pounds) mussels, with shell
300 g (10 oz) (10 ounces) carrots
2 medium onions
2 small leeks
1 celeriac, or 5 sticks celery
30 g (1 oz) (2 tbs) butter
1 tbs (½ tbs) (½ tbs) flour
freshly ground pepper
salt
finely chopped parsley or celery leaves, to garnish

1. Scrub the mussels thoroughly in cold running
water and trim away the beards. Discard any which
are already open. Cook them for 10 minutes in ¾ l
(1¼ pts) (3 cups) water and throw away any which
fail to open. Remove the mussels from the shells
and strain the liquid for the soup.
2. Peel and thinly slice the carrots. Peel and chop
the onions or slice into rings.
3. Wash the leeks thoroughly and slice thinly. Peel
and chop the celeriac into small cubes.
4. Heat the butter in a large heavy based pan and
sauté the carrots, onions, leeks and celery for 7
minutes or until soft. Stir in the flour a couple of
minutes before the end of the cooking time.
5. Make the cooking liquid from the mussels up to 1
l (1¾ pts) (4 cups) with water, stir into the sautéed
vegetables and bring slowly to the boil, stirring all
the time.
6. Season to taste with salt and pepper, add the
cooked mussels just before serving and garnish with
chopped parsley and celery leaves.

Broccoli soup

(Broccolisoep)

approx. 600 g (1¼ lb) (1¼ pounds) broccoli
1 medium onion
1 leek
2 tomatoes
100 g (4 oz) (2 cups) button mushrooms
60 g (2 oz) (4 tbs) butter
8 dl (1¼ pts) (3¼ cups) vegetable or chicken stock
(see p. 17)
2 dl (7 fl oz) (¾ cup) milk
2 egg yolks
1 dl (3½ fl oz) (⅓ cup) cream
salt
freshly ground pepper

2 drops Worcestershire sauce
1 tbs (½ tbs) (½ tbs) tomato ketchup
finely chopped parsley or chives to garnish

1. Wash the broccoli and divide it into rosettes. Slice the stalks thinly.
2. Peel and finely chop the onion. Wash the leek thoroughly and chop it finely. Blanch the tomatoes for 10 seconds in boiling water, peel them, remove the seeds and finely chop the flesh.
3. Wipe the mushrooms and trim the base of the stalks.
4. Heat the butter in a large heavy based pan and sauté the onion and leek until soft. Add the tomatoes and the sliced broccoli stalks and sauté for a further 3 minutes.
5. Heat the stock and milk in a separate pan and

Broccoli soup not only tastes delicious, it is also a very attractive soup.

stir into the sautéed vegetables.

6. Add the broccoli rosettes and bring the soup to the boil. Cover the pan and simmer gently for about 20 minutes.

7. Add the mushrooms 5 minutes before the end of the cooking time – halve large mushrooms if necessary.

8. Blend the egg yolks with the cream in a small bowl and stir into the soup. Heat through gently, stirring all the time, but do not bring the soup back to the boil.

9. Season with salt, pepper, Worcestershire sauce and tomato ketchup, garnish with chopped parsley and serve with croutons or fresh triangles of toast.

Lamb soup with turnips

(Reubesoep uit Limburg)

250-300 g (8-10 oz) (8-10 ounces) lamb or mutton
1 tsp (½ tsp) (½ tsp) dried thyme
1 tsp (½ tsp) (½ tsp) dried rosemary
4 peppercorns
500 g (1 lb) (1 pound) young turnips
5 small carrots, 2-3 potatoes
75 g (3 oz) (3 ounces) streaky bacon
finely chopped parsley to garnish

1. Cut the meat into 2 cm (1 inch) cubes and bring to the boil with at least 1 l (1¾ pts) (4 cups) of water in a large heavy based pan. Add the thyme, rosemary and lightly crushed peppercorns and skim the surface of the soup.

2. Cover the pan and simmer gently for at least 3 hours.

3. Prepare the vegetables 30 minutes before the end of the cooking time. Peel and chop the young turnips, or cut into thin slices, peel and chop the carrots, peel and chop the potatoes or grate them on a coarse grater.

4. Add the vegetables to the soup 15 minutes before the end of the cooking time and cook until tender but firm to the bite (al dente).

5. Cut the bacon into small cubes or wafer thin slices and fry until golden brown in its own fat. Garnish the soup with the fried bacon and chopped parsley and serve piping hot.

Beef and vegetable soup

(Humkes-(of Hummekes)soep uit Twente)

A hearty soup from the eastern Dutch province of Twente.

200 g (7 oz) (1¼ cups) haricot beans
250 g (8 oz) (8 ounces) shin of beef
500 g (1 lb) (1 pound) brisket
salt
1 tsp (½ tsp) (½ tsp) peppercorns
3-4 cloves
1 bay leaf
½ celeriac or 3 sticks celery
3 large potatoes
3 medium onions
1 leek
200 g (7 oz) (7 ounces) runner or French beans
1 small bunch parsley

1. Soak the haricot beans overnight in ½ l (1 pt) (2 cups) water.

2. Bring the shin of beef and the brisket to the boil with 1 l (1¾ pts) (4 cups) water and skim the surface.

3. Add salt to taste, the lightly crushed peppercorns, cloves and bay leaf, cover and simmer gently for 1½ hours.

4. Stir in the soaked haricot beans, together with the water in which they were soaked and simmer the soup for another hour.

5. Meanwhile, peel the celeriac and the potatoes and cut into even sized cubes or chop the celery stalks.

6. Peel and finely chop the onions. Rinse and slice the runner beans or chop the French beans into small pieces.

7. Add the celeriac, potatoes, onions and beans to the soup and simmer gently for a further 25 minutes or until the vegetables are tender.

8. Remove the brisket from the pan and cut into manageable sized pieces – serve on a separate plate.

9. Garnish the soup with freshly chopped parsley and serve with the sliced brisket and a basket of rough brown or granary bread.

Bean soup with bacon

(Bruine-bonensoep)

250 g (8 oz) (8 ounces) dried kidney beans
1 bay leaf
2 cloves
300 g (10 oz) (10 ounces) streaky bacon, cut into
3 slices
1 medium onion
2 small leeks
2 medium potatoes
1 stalk celery, chopped
2 sprigs parsley
salt
freshly ground pepper

1. Wash the kidney beans and soak them overnight in 1½ l (2¾ pts) (6 cups) water. Bring them to the boil (in the water in which they were soaked) and add the bay leaf, the cloves and the bacon. Cover the pan and simmer gently for 1 hour or until the beans are soft.
2. Peel and finely chop the onion, wash the leeks, halve lengthwise and slice thinly.
3. Peel the potatoes and cut into small cubes.
4. Wash and finely chop the parsley.
5. Remove the bayleaf and cloves, remove the beans from the cooking liquid and rub them through a sieve or puree in a food processor. Return to the pan.
6. Add the onion, leeks, potatoes, celery and parsley to the soup and simmer gently for a further 25 minutes.
7. Remove the bacon from the soup and cut into cubes. Stir them back into the soup and serve with rye bread (pumpernickel) or rough brown bread and butter.

Dutch pea soup

(Erwtensoep)

500 g (1 lb) (1 pound) split peas
300 g (10 oz) (10 ounces) spareribs, pork brisket or pig's trotters, or a mixture of these meats
250 g (8 oz) (8 ounces) streaky bacon
500 g (1 lb) (1 pound) leeks
1 celeriac or 5 stalks celery, chopped
1 large carrot
6 sprigs celery leaves or parsley
1 cooked smoked boiling sausage, approx. 300 g (10 oz) (10 ounces)
salt
freshly ground pepper

1. Rinse the split peas and soak for a few hours in cold water. Drain well.
2. Bring the split peas, spareribs (or other meat) and cubed bacon to the boil with approximately 2 l (3¼ pts) (8 cups) water.
3. Meanwhile, wash and slice the leeks fairly thickly.
4. Peel the celeriac and cut into small cubes.
5. Peel the carrot and cut into cubes or slices.
6. Wash the celery leaves or parsley, chop half and reserve for the garnish.
7. Stir the prepared vegetables and whole celery leaves or parsley to the soup and season with salt and pepper to taste. Cover the pan and simmer for at least 2 hours, or until the meat is tender. Stir the soup occasionally and add a little extra water if necessary.
8. Remove the spareribs (or other meat) from the pan, discard the bones and chop the flesh.
9. Return the chopped meat to the soup, add the sliced boiling sausage and garnish with a little chopped celery leaves or parsley. Serve with rye bread (pumpernickel), sliced French bread or fresh toast.

Note:
If smoked boiling sausage (rookworst) is not available, use an equivalent weight of Frankfurter sausages.

Dutch pea soup. This hearty winter soup is easy to prepare.

Mayonnaise

(Mayonaise)

2 egg yolks
salt
freshly ground white pepper
1 tsp (½ tsp) (½ tsp) dry mustard
3 dl (½ pt) (1¼ cup) sunflower oil
2 tbs (1½ tbs) (1½ tbs) herb vinegar

1. Beat the egg yolks with the salt, pepper and mustard in a small, deep bowl.
2. Add the oil drop by drop, whisking vigourously between each addition of oil so that it is completely absorbed. As the mayonnaise thickens and becomes shiny, the oil may be added in a thin stream.
3. Blend the vinegar into the mayonnaise and check the seasoning.
4. Serve mayonnaise with cold meat, fish, shellfish, eggs, and raw and cooked vegetables.
5. For a thicker mayonnaise, add a little more oil – extra vinegar or lemon juice will make the mayonnaise thinner.

Tip:
Mayonnaise will keep for up to a week in the refrigerator, if it is stored in a jar with a well fitting lid.

Variation:
Vary the flavour by adding 1-2 tablespoons of finely chopped parsley, dill or chives just before serving. The mayonnaise can then be used as a dip sauce or as an accompaniment to all types of hot and cold fish dishes.

Home made mayonnaise always tastes better than the ready made variety.

Cocktail sauce

(Cocktailsaus)

1 dl (3½ fl oz) (½ cup) cream or sour cream
1 dl (3½ fl oz) (½ cup) tomato ketchup
1½ tbs (1 tbs) (1 tbs) mayonnaise (see p. 26)
1 tbs (½ tbs) (½ tbs) lemon juice or wine vinegar
2 tbs (1½ tbs) (1½ tbs) brandy or sherry
salt
freshly ground pepper

1. Chill all the ingredients, except for the mayonnaise for at least an hour before preparing the sauce.
2. Lightly whip the fresh cream and stir in the remaining ingredients to make a smooth, creamy sauce.

Tip:
A delicious sauce to use with a fish cocktail, prawn or crab cocktail for example, or with Dutch herring salad (see p. 12).

Rich butter sauce

(Botersaus)

100 g (4 oz) (½ cup) butter
30 g (1 oz) (3 tbs) flour
5 dl (17 fl oz) (2 cups) meat, fish or vegetable stock
(see p. 16 and 17)
salt
freshly ground pepper

1. Melt half of the butter in a heavy based pan.
2. Add the flour and cook gently over a low heat, stirring all the time.
3. Gradually stir in the (hot) stock to make a smooth sauce and cook gently for about 5 minutes, stirring occasionally.
4. Season carefully with salt and freshly ground pepper and beat in the remaining butter.
5. Reheat the sauce if necessary before serving, but do not bring it back to the boil.

Béchamel sauce

(Béchamelsaus)

50 g (2 oz) (4 tbs) butter
50 g (2 oz) (6 tbs) flour
4-5 dl (14-17 fl oz) (1¾ – 2 cups) milk
salt

1. Melt the butter in a small heavy based pan and add the flour. Cook gently for 2-3 minutes, stirring all the time.
2. Meanwhile, heat the milk in a separate pan. Gradually stir the warm milk into the roux, bring to the boil, stirring continuously, then simmer for 2 -3 minutes to make a smooth, thick sauce.
3. The thickness of the sauce depends on how it is to be used. Add less milk for a thick, coating sauce, or more milk for a thinner, pouring sauce.

Cornflour sauce

(Bloemkoolsaus)

20 g (¾ oz) (2 tbs) cornflour or cornstarch
2½ dl (8 fl oz) (1 cup) milk
20 g (¾ oz) (1½ tbs) butter
salt
freshly ground pepper

1. Blend the cornflour with 3 tablespoons of the cold milk and heat the rest of the milk in a heavy based pan.
2. Stir the cornflour blend into the milk as it reaches boiling point and lower the heat.
3. Simmer the sauce for 2 minutes, stir in the butter and season to taste with salt and pepper.

Tip:
Add a pinch of ground nutmeg and serve the sauce with cauliflower, broccoli or white or green cabbage.

Brown sauce

(Bruine saus)

40 g (1½ oz) (1½ ounces) streaky bacon
40 g (1½ oz) (3 tbs) butter
1 small onion
100 g (4 oz) (4 ounces) carrot
1 stick celery, finely chopped
1 sprig parsley
pinch thyme
1 small bay leaf
40 g (1½ oz) (4 tbs) flour
7-8 dl (1¼-1½ pts) (3-3½ cups) meat stock
½ dl (4 tbs) (4 tbs) red wine

1. Cut the bacon into small cubes or thin slices.
2. Melt the butter in a heavy based pan.
3. Peel and finely chop the onion. Scrape and finely chop the carrot.
4. Sauté the onion in the hot butter until it is golden brown, add the chopped carrot and fry gently for a few more minutes.
5. Wash and dry the parsley and chop it finely. Add them to the sautéed vegetables, together with the thyme and the crumbled bay leaf. Fry gently until all the ingredients are golden brown.
6. Drain off half of the bacon fat and stir the flour into the ingredients in the pan.
7. Cook gently for 2-3 minutes before adding the (warm) stock and the wine.
8. Boil fiercely until the sauce has reduced to two-thirds of it's original volume. Add a little tomato ketchup or chilli sauce for a piquanter flavour.

Béarnaise sauce – Choron sauce

(Béarnaisesaus-Choronsaus)

2 shallots or 1 medium onion
1 dl (3½ fl oz) (½ cup) white wine vinegar
1 dl (3½ fl oz) (½ cup) dry white wine
6-8 peppercorns
1 tbs (½ tbs) (½ tbs) each finely chopped parsley,
tarragon and chervil
3 egg yolks
200 g (8 oz) (1 cup) butter
lemon juice
1 tsp (½ tsp)(½ tsp)
1 tsp (1 tsp) (1 tsp) each finely chopped tarragon and
chervil
salt
freshly ground pepper

1. Peel and finely chop the shallots or onion. Put them into a heavy based pan, together with the vinegar, white wine and lightly crushed peppercorns. Stir in the parsley, tarragon and chervil.
2. Bring to the boil and then simmer gently until the liquid has reduced to approximately 1 dl (3½ fl oz) (½ cup). Strain through a fine sieve.
3. Beat the egg yolks in a small basin and gradually add the (cooled) reduced liquid.
4. Heat the mixture au bain marie, whisking all the time to make a smooth, thick sauce.
5. Cut the butter into small pieces and stir them into the hot sauce, one at a time.
6. Season the Bearnaise sauce with lemon juice, tarragon, chervil, salt and freshly ground pepper.

Variation:
Stir in 1-2 tablespoons of tomato ketchup to make a delicious Choron sauce.

Tip:
Both sauces are ideal accompaniments to roast and grilled meats or cold cuts of beef, pork, veal or lamb.

Hollandaise sauce

(Hollandse saus)

1 tbs (½ tbs) (½ tbs) herb vinegar
2 egg yolks
salt
freshly ground white pepper
200 g (8 oz) (1 cup) butter
1 tbs (½ tbs) (½ tbs) lemon juice

1. Bring the vinegar and 1 dl (3½ fl oz) (½ cup) water to the boil in a small non-aluminium saucepan. Reduce until it is half of it's original volume. This will neutralise the sharp flavour of the vinegar a little.
2. Beat the egg yolks in a small bowl with the cooled, reduced vinegar and transfer to a bain-marie or place the bowl over a pan of simmering water.
3. Stir until the sauce begins to thicken; the water in the bain-marie must not be allowed to boil.
4. Season to taste with salt and pepper and cut the butter into small pieces. Stir the pieces of butter into the sauce, one by one. Allow sufficient time for each to melt before adding the next one.
5. Beat well until the sauce is smooth and thick.
6. Warm a sauce boat, season the Hollandaise with the lemon juice and serve luke-warm.

Variation:
Add 3-4 tablespoons of lightly whipped cream to get Mousseline sauce.

Three delicious sauces: from left to right – Cocktail sauce (p. 27), Hollandaise sauce (see above) and Choron sauce (p. 28).

Onion sauce

(Uiensaus)

2-3 medium onions
1 clove garlic (optional)
40 g (1½ oz) (3 tbs) butter
sugar to taste
40 g (1½ oz) (4 tbs) flour
5 dl (17 fl oz) (2 cups) meat or chicken stock
1 tbs (½ tbs) (½ tbs) wine vinegar
1 tbs (½ tbs)(½ tbs) lemon juice
salt
freshly ground black pepper
pinch ground bay leaves

1. Peel and finely chop the onions and add a crushed clove of garlic for extra flavour if wished.
2. Heat the butter in a heavy based pan and sauté the onion until soft. Stir in a little sugar to taste and the sifted flour. Cook gently for 2-3 minutes, stirring continuously.
3. Gradually stir in the (hot) stock, wine vinegar and lemon juice.
4. Season to taste with salt, pepper and ground bay leaves. Simmer gently for about 7 minutes before serving.

Tip:
Use a non-aluminium pan as the acid ingredients (vinegar and lemon juice) may damage the surface of the pan,which may give the sauce a peculiar taste.

Variation:
Vary the flavour by adding 1-2 tbs of tomato ketchup and/or 1-2 tsp made mustard or ½ – 1 tsp minced horseradish cream (available in tubes or jars at delicatessens).
Use finely chopped spring onions (scallions) instead of ordinary ones and sauté for just a minute in the hot butter.

Parsley sauce

(Peterseliesaus)

50 g (2 oz)(4 tbs) butter
50 g (2 oz) (6 tbs) flour
5 dl (17 fl oz) (2 cups) stock
1-2 tbs (½-1 tbs)(½-1 tbs) finely chopped parsley
salt
freshly ground pepper

1. Melt the butter in a heavy based saucepan.
2. Stir in the flour and cook gently for 2-3 minutes.
3. Gradually add the (hot) stock, stirring all the time, to make a smooth, thick sauce and simmer gently for 4 minutes.
4. Add the parsley and season with salt and white or black pepper.

Variation:
Use finely chopped chives or dill instead of the parsley and serve with steamed, fried or baked fish.

Egg sauce

(Eiersaus)

50 g (2 oz) (4 tbs) butter
50 g (2 oz) (6 tbs) flour
5 dl (17 fl oz) (2 cups) stock
a little finely chopped parsley
3 small eggs
1 tbs (½ tbs) (½ tbs) wine or herb vinegar
salt
freshly ground white pepper

1. Follow the instructions for the parsley sauce, but add a little less parsley.
2. Beat the eggs with 1 tablespoon of water and pour the hot sauce over the beaten eggs, stirring all the time.
3. Season to taste with vinegar, salt and pepper. Return the mixture to the pan and heat the sauce for 2 minutes, without bringing it to the boil and stirring all the time. If it boils the eggs may curdle and spoil the sauce.

Tomato sauce

(Tomatensaus)

1 kg (2 lb) (2 pounds) ripe tomatoes
4 shallots or 2 onions
2 small carrots
50 g (2 oz) (4 tbs) butter
1 tbs (½ tbs) (½ tbs) finely chopped parsley
½ finely chopped stick celery
2 tbs (1½ tbs) (1½ tbs) flour
3 tbs (2 tbs) (2 tbs) stock
2 tbs (1½ tbs) (1½ tbs) red wine
pinch dried basil
pinch oregano
salt
freshly ground black pepper
1 tsp (½ tsp) (½ tsp) caster sugar

1. Blanch the tomatoes for 10 seconds in boiling water, peel and finely chop them or puree in a blender or food processor.
2. Peel and finely chop the shallots; scrape and finely chop the carrots.
3. Heat the butter in a fairly large heavy based saucepan and sauté the shallots and carrots for a few minutes. Add the tomatoes and stir well. Cover the pan and simmer the contents for about 20 minutes.
4. Add the parsley and celery and stir in the flour.
5. Mix the stock with the red wine and stir into the sauce, together with the basil, oregano, salt, pepper and sugar to taste.
6. Simmer the tomato sauce in the uncovered pan for a further 10 minutes or until it is fairly thick.

Treacle sauce

(Stroopsaus)

40 g (1½ oz) (4 tbs) flour
5 dl (17 fl oz) (2 cups) milk
40 g (1½ oz) (3 tbs) butter
3 dl (½ pt) (1¼ cups) treacle, syrup or molasses

1. Blend the flour with one-third of the milk and bring the rest of the milk to the boil in a small, heavy based pan.
2. Stir the blended flour into the hot milk, bring it back to the boil and then simmer gently for 3-4 minutes, stirring occasionally. Cut the butter into small pieces and stir them into the sauce, one by one.
3. Remove the pan from the heat, cool for 5 minutes and then gradually add the treacle, syrup or molasses, stirring until it is thoroughly blended into the sauce.

Tip:
A delicious sauce to serve with hot or cold rice pudding, pancakes, poor knights (strips of bread soaked in egg and milk and then fried) or ice cream.

Vanilla sauce

(Vanillesaus)

5 dl (17 fl oz) (2 cups) milk
¼ vanilla pod or 1 tbs vanilla sugar*
salt
2-3 egg yolks
2½ tbs (2 tbs) (2 tbs) caster sugar
2 tsp (1½ tsp) (1½ tsp) cornflour or cornstarch

1. Bring the milk to the boil in a heavy based saucepan with the vanilla pod and a pinch of salt. Remove the pan from the heat and allow to draw for about 12 minutes.
2. Beat the egg yolks lightly with the sugar and the cornflour and blend with a few spoonfuls of the hot milk.
3. Stir this blend into the remaining milk in the pan and bring slowly to the boil, stirring all the time.
4. Cook for 1 minute, until the sauce has thickened, remove the vanilla pod and serve hot or cold.

* Add the vanilla sugar to the blended egg yolks

31

Chocolate sauce

(Chocoladesaus)

200 g (8 oz) (8 ounces) plain chocolate
3½ dl (12 fl oz) (1½ cups) water
3 tbs (2 tbs) (2 tbs) coffee liqueur
1 tbs (½ tbs) (½ tbs) barbados sugar
1 egg yolk
5 tbs (4 tbs) (4 tbs) lightly soured cream

1. Break the chocolate into small pieces and place them with the water in a bain-marie pan or in a small bowl over a pan of hot water. Stir until the chocolate has melted.
2. Stir in the coffee liqueur, barbados sugar, lightly beaten egg yolk and sour cream to make a rich, thick sauce.

Blueberry sauce

(Bosbessensaus)

400 g (14 oz) (14 ounces) blueberries
2 cloves
1 stick cinnamon
the peel from a well scrubbed lemon
1 tbs (½ tbs) (½ tbs) arrowroot or potato flour
2 tbs (1½ tbs) (1½ tbs) berry liqueur
50 g (2 oz) (2 ounces) caster sugar

1. Top and tail the blueberries and rinse them in a colander. Pulp them in a juice extractor or puree them in an electric blender or food processor and put the sauce into a small saucepan, together with 1 dl (3½ fl oz) (½ cup) water, the cloves, cinnamon stick and lemon peel.
2. Bring to the boil, remove the pan from the heat and leave to draw for 30 minutes. Strain the blueberry juice. Blend the arrowroot with a little of the cooled juice, bring the remaining juice back to the boil and thicken with the arrowroot blend.
3. Stir in the liqueur and the sugar and leave the sauce to cool. Serve with hot or cold desserts e.g. bread pudding, fruit sorbets, ice sundaes and blancmange or custard.

Strawberry sauce

(Aardbeiensaus)

500 g (1 lb) (1 pound) ripe strawberries
1 lemon
2 tbs (1½ tbs) (1½ tbs) honey
2 tsp (1½ tsp) (1½ tsp) vanilla sugar
approx. 2½ tbs (2 tbs) (2 tbs) caster sugar

1. Pick over the strawberries and keep 4 perfect ones to use as a garnish.
2. Wash the remaining fruit, remove the crowns and puree them in an electric blender or food processor with the juice of the lemon, honey, vanilla sugar and caster sugar.
3. Pour the sauce into a chilled sauce boat and garnish with the whole strawberries.

Orange sauce

(Sinaasappelsaus)

4 well scrubbed oranges
4-5 sugar lumps
1 lemon
1 tbs (½ tbs) (½ tbs) arrowroot or potato starch
1 tbs (½ tbs) (½ tbs) Grand Marnier
2½ tbs (2 tbs) (2 tbs) caster sugar

1. Remove the zest from the oranges by rubbing them with the sugar lumps, or grate the peel as finely as possible.
2. Squeeze out the juice or pulp them in a juice extractor and make the juice up to 3½ dl (12 fl oz) (1½ cups) with water. Heat the juice gently.
3. Squeeze the lemon and blend the arrowroot with the juice. Use this to thicken the hot orange juice, add the liqueur and sugar and stir until the sugar has dissolved and the sauce has thickened slightly. Add the finely grated orange peel or use the sugar lumps to sweeten the sauce instead of the caster sugar and leave the sauce to cool.

Tip:
Serve this tangy orange sauce with vanilla custard, hot or cold rice pudding or semolina mould.

Top left: Orange sauce; Bottom left: Blueberry sauce; Right: Strawberry sauce.

Cheese and Eggs

Poached eggs

(Gepocheerde eieren)

2 tbs (1 tbs) (1 tbs) vinegar
1 tsp (1 tsp) (1 tsp) salt
8 very fresh eggs

1. Bring 2-3 l (3-5 pts) (8-12 cups) water to the boil in a shallow pan, approximately 24 cm (10 inches) in diameter. Add the vinegar and the salt.
2. Reduce the heat to simmering point.
3. Break the eggs, one at a time, into a small cup and slide them into the simmering water, taking care that they do not touch the bottom of the pan.
4. Poach the eggs for approximately 4 minutes, adjusting the heat if necessary to ensure that the water remains at simmering point. Remove them from the pan with a perforated spoon and trim the whites to a neat shape.
5. Serve on hot buttered toast, use as a garnish for clear soup or coat with cheese sauce and brown under a hot grill for a light lunch dish. Cold poached eggs can also be served as a starter with Mayonnaise, Bearnaise or Choron sauce (see p. 28). Garnish with a dusting of ground paprika or finely chopped garden herbs.

Tip:
Use a commercial egg poaching pan for a perfectly shaped poached egg. Follow the manufacturer's instructions and serve as above.

Country style omelette

(Boerenomelet)

5 medium sized eggs
75 g (3 oz) (3 ounces) streaky bacon
1 onion
1 clove garlic
1 small leek
½ large carrot or 3 small ones
6 mushrooms
2 tomatoes
3 tbs (2 tbs) (2 tbs) stock, home made or from a cube
pinch freshly ground black pepper
finely chopped garden herbs (chervil, chives, parsley etc.)
2 tbs (1½ tbs) (1½ tbs) cooked peas

1. Lightly beat the eggs in a large bowl.
2. Snip the bacon into small pieces.
3. Peel and finely chop the onion and garlic.
4. Clean and chop the leek and carrot(s).
5. Wipe the mushrooms with a damp cloth, but do not immerse them in water, otherwise they will absorb some of the water and then shrink during cooking.
6. Sauté the bacon in a large non-stick frying pan (24 cm) (12 inches) in diameter) until it is soft.
7. Add the onion, garlic and leek and fry gently for 2-3 minutes.
8. Stir in the carrot(s) and sliced mushrooms and fry gently for a further 2-3 minutes.
9. Blanch the tomatoes for 10 seconds in boiling water, remove the peel, scoop out the seeds and chop the flesh in small pieces. Stir them into the sautéed vegetables and fry gently whilst you prepare the eggs.
10. Whisk the stock, pepper and finely chopped garden herbs into the beaten eggs, stir in the peas and pour into the pan. Tip the pan slightly to ensure that the egg mixture evenly coats the sautéed vegetables, cover with a lid and cook over a low heat until the surface of the omelette appears dry.
11. Slide the omelette onto a warm, flat plate and serve with rough brown or granary bread.

Country style omelette with bacon and vegetables, seasoned with fresh garden herbs.

Birds' nests

(Vogelnestjes)

6 medium eggs
1 tbs (½ tbs)(½ tbs) cream
approx. 150 g (6 oz) (6 ounces) cold roast meat
a few cocktail onions
2 tsp (1½ tsp) (1½ tsp) finely chopped parsley
1 stick celery, finely chopped
2-3 small gherkins or sweet pickles
salt
freshly ground pepper
pinch ground nutmeg
50 g (2 oz) (4 tbs) butter
few sprigs parsley for the garnish
1 well scrubbed lemon

1. Lightly beat two of the eggs with the cream in a medium sized bowl.
2. Chop the cold meat into small pieces or mince it coarsely.
3. Stir the meat, drained cocktail onions, parsley, celery and finely chopped gherkins into the beaten eggs.
4. Season with salt, pepper and nutmeg to taste.
5. Melt the butter in a large frying pan and remove the pan from the heat. Divide the meat mixture into four and spoon each portion into the frying pan. Make an indentation in the top of each mound, with the back of a spoon.
6. Break an egg into each hollow, taking care that the egg white doesn't flow over the edge. Fry gently until the egg white has completely set.
7. Serve the birds' nests on a warm flat plate or in individual dishes and garnish each with a sprig of parsley and a slice of lemon.

Boiled eggs with green sauce

(Eieren in groene saus)

8 medium eggs
2 dl (7 fl oz) (⅞ cup) Bulgarian yoghurt
1½ dl (5 fl oz) (⅔ cup) lightly soured cream
salt
freshly ground white pepper
4 tbs (3 tbs) (3 tbs) finely chopped garden herbs
(parsley, chervil, chives, tarragon, basil etc.)
3 tbs (2 tbs) (2 tbs) lemon or lime juice
1 tsp (½ tsp)(½ tsp) caster sugar
½ cucumber
2 tomatoes

1. Boil the eggs for 10 minutes, plunge them into cold water and remove the shells. Cut each in half lengthwise and arrange them on a special egg plate (with indentations) or cut a small slice from the base of each half and arrange them on a large, flat plate.
2. Beat the yoghurt with the soured cream, season with salt and pepper to taste and add the finely chopped garden herbs.
3. Stir in the lemon or lime juice and a little sugar to taste and chill the sauce in the refrigerator.
4. Meanwhile, wash the cucumber and the tomatoes, cut the cucumber in half lengthwise and then across in thin slices.
5. Halve the tomatoes, scoop out the seeds and juice and finely chop the tomato flesh.
6. Pour the chilled sauce over the eggs, garnish with cucumber and spoon the chopped tomatoes over the top.

Tip:
A delicious snack or cocktail titbit. The eggs can be boiled and shelled in advance and then kept in a bowl of cold water in the refrigerator.
Sharpen the sauce by adding a few drops of Worcestershire sauce or tabasco.

Savoury stuffed meatballs

(Eieren in gehakt)

see photo on page 38-39.

400 g (14 oz) (14 ounces) lean mince
salt, freshly ground pepper and ground nutmeg
1 onion
1 small leek
1 red pepper
4 button mushrooms
25 g (1 oz) (2 tbs) butter
4 hard boiled eggs
2 egg whites
dried breadcrumbs

1. Break up the mince with a fork and season with salt, pepper and a little nutmeg. Peel and finely chop the onion. Clean and thinly slice the leek.
2. Wash the red pepper, cut it in half, remove the seeds and white pith and chop into small cubes.
3. Wipe the mushrooms clean with kitchen paper and slice thinly.
4. Heat the butter in a frying pan and sauté the onion and leek until soft. Add the pepper and mushrooms and fry gently for 2-3 minutes. Allow the mixture to cool and knead it into the seasoned mince.
5. Shell the eggs and divide the mince into 4 portions. Shape each piece into a ball, make a hollow in the centre and place the egg into the hollow.
6. Mould the mince around the egg, making sure that there are no cracks in the surface.
7. Coat each meatball first with beaten egg white and then with dried breadcrumbs. Deep fry the meatballs golden brown in hot oil or fat, drain on kitchen paper and serve hot or cold.

Oven baked cheese rolls

(Kaasbroodjes uit de oven)

4 soft wholemeal rolls
25 g (1 oz) (2 tbs) butter
8 slices Dutch cheese, about 20 g (¾ oz) (¾ ounce) each
16 thin slices salami
4 slices tomato
4 leaves iceberg lettuce
4 sprigs parsley

1. Preheat the oven to 220 °C (425 °F). Split the rolls and spread with a little butter.
2. Top each half with 1 slice of cheese and 2 slices of salami.
3. Place 1 slice of tomato and 1 lettuce leaf on four of the halved rolls and cover with the remaining halves.
4. Arrange the filled rolls on a baking sheet and bake for 8-10 minutes at the top of the oven or until the rolls are crisp and the cheese has melted.
5. Garnish each with a sprig of parsley.

Photo on following pages: Savoury stuffed meatballs – easy to make with surprising results.

Dutch cheese fondue

(Kaasdoop uit Zuid-Holland)

A delicious creamy cheese fondue from the south of Holland. Dutch Gouda cheese is particularly good for making fondues as it has a high fat content and melts easily. Use a fairly young Dutch Gouda cheese – most of the cheese exported from Holland is young. Look out for the marking on the rind of the cheese; it will give you some indication as to the maturity of the cheese.

5 dl (17 fl oz) (2 cups) milk
approx. 350 g (12 oz) (4½ cups) grated young or
semi-matured Dutch cheese
20 g (¾ oz) (2 tbs) cornflour or cornstarch
2-3 tbs (1-2 tbs) (1-2 tbs) Dutch brandy (brandewijn)
or kirsch
freshly ground pepper
pinch nutmeg
wholemeal or granary bread

1. Bring the milk to the boil in a fondue pan or heavy based saucepan and gradually stir in the cheese. Remove the pan from the heat and continue stirring until the cheese has melted.
2. Blend the cornflour with the brandy or kirsch and stir the blend into the fondue sauce.
3. Season with pepper and nutmeg. Place the pan on a rechaud.
4. Cut the bread into 2 cm (1 inch) cubes and serve with the fondue. Use long fondue forks to dip the chunks of bread into the sauce.
5. Serve with dry white wine or cold lager.

Dutch style bacon and eggs

(Spiegeleieren met kaas en spek)

butter for frying
8 thin rashers streaky bacon
4 eggs
4 slices Dutch cheese (young or semi-mature)
freshly ground black pepper
salt
1 tomato
4 lettuce leaves

1. Melt the butter in a large heavy based frying pan.
2. Lightly fry the slices of bacon and then arrange them in a single layer over the base of the pan.
3. Break the eggs into the pan on top of the bacon.
4. Cover each egg with a slice of cheese and cook over a gently heat until the egg white has set – the yolks should still be runny.
5. Serve the bacon and eggs on buttered bread and season with a little pepper and salt.
6. Garnish each portion with a slice of tomato and a fresh lettuce leaf and eat piping hot.

Cheese pudding

(Broodschotel met kaas en ei)

butter
2-3 medium eggs
4 tbs (3 tbs) (3 tbs) cream
3 dl (½ pt) (1¼ cups) milk
1 dl (3½ fl oz) (½ cup) yoghurt
salt
freshly ground pepper
2 tbs (1 tbs) (1 tbs) lemon juice
1 tbs (½ tbs) (½ tbs) stem ginger syrup
8 thin slices white or brown bread, cut from a
square loaf
200 g (8 oz) (8 ounces) sliced Dutch cheese
2 tbs (1 tbs) (1 tbs) dried breadcrumbs

1. Lightly butter an ovenproof soufflé dish.
2. Beat the eggs with the cream, milk and yoghurt and season with salt, pepper, lemon juice and ginger syrup.
3. Soak the slices of bread, one by one in the egg mixture and layer them up with the cheese in the buttered soufflé dish.
4. Sprinkle the dried breadcrumbs on top and dot with flakes of butter.
5. Bake for 30 minutes in a preheated oven (200°C) (400°F) or until the top is crisp and golden brown.

Tip:
Serve as a snack or savoury supper dish. This also makes a delicious light lunch dish when served with clear chicken soup and a fresh green salad!

Scrambled eggs with cress

(Roereieren met sterkers)

See photo on page 42-43.

6 eggs
4 tbs (3 tbs) (3 tbs) milk
2 tbs (1 tbs) (1 tbs) cream
salt
freshly ground black pepper
25 g (1 oz) (2 tbs) butter
1 small punnet cress

1. Lightly beat the eggs with the milk, cream, salt and pepper to taste in a large bowl.
2. Melt the butter in a medium sized saucepan, preferably with a non-stick surface and add the beaten egg mixture.
3. Reduce the heat and stir until the eggs have just set – the surface should still be a little moist.
4. Serve the scrambled eggs on warm plates with brown or white rolls and garnish with cress and radishes if desired.

On following pages: scrambled eggs with cress.

Soufflé omelette with cheese

(Schuimomelet met kaas)

4-5 eggs
approx. 50 g (2 oz) (²⁄₃ cup) grated mature cheese
2 tbs (1½ tbs) (1½ tbs) finely chopped parsley
1 tbs (½ tbs)(½ tbs) light stock
1 tbs (½ tbs)(½ tbs) thin cream
salt
freshly ground pepper
pinch ground nutmeg
pinch curry powder
60 g (2 oz) (2 ounces) streaky bacon
butter or oil for frying

1. Separate the eggs and beat the egg yolks with the grated cheese, parsley stock and cream.
2. Season to taste with salt, pepper, nutmeg and curry powder.
3. Beat the egg whites with a pinch of salt until they are stiff and dry and fold them into the egg yolk mixture.
4. Cut the bacon into thin strips and fry them golden brown in a little butter or oil.
5. Heat a knob of butter or a spoonful of oil in a separate pan, pour in the egg mixture and cover with a lightly greased, well fitting lid. Cook the omelette for about 8 minutes over a low heat or until the underside is golden brown and the top set, but still a little moist.
6. Spoon the strips of bacon over the omelette, fold it in half and serve on a warm, flat plate.

Tip:
Serve this tasty omelette with potato croquettes, røsti, fried potatoes or hot French bread or rolls.

Savoury cheese butter

(Kaasboter)

250 g (8 oz) (1 cup) soft butter
9-10 hard boiled eggs
salt
freshly ground white pepper
pinch curry powder
1 tbs (½ tbs) (½ tbs) tomato ketchup
2 drops Worcestershire sauce
approx. 60 g (2 oz) (²⁄₃ cup) grated cheese
1 tbs (½ tbs) (½ tbs) finely chopped parsley

1. Beat the butter in a small mixing bowl. Shell the eggs, cut them in half and scoop out the yolks. Beat the yolks one by one into the butter.
2. Season with salt, pepper, curry powder, tomato ketchup and Worcestershire sauce.
3. Stir in the grated cheese and the parsley and spoon the mixture into a piping bag fitted with a fluted nozzle. Pipe a little of the cheese butter into each of the egg whites or use as a filling for choux pastry puffs, individual pastry cases, celery sticks, cucumber (seeds scooped out), small red or green peppers etc.

Tip:
For a quick snack, this delicious savoury butter can also simply be spread on crackers or melba toast.

Pickled herrings

(Zure haring)

8 fresh herrings
2 medium onions
2 bay leaves
1 lemon or about 10 gherkins
2 tsp (1½ tsp) (1½ tsp) peppercorns
vinegar

1. Thoroughly clean a preserving jar with a solution of soda, rinse with boiling water and drain upside down on a clean tea towel.
2. Clean the herrings, rinse them well and then soak overnight in plenty of cold water.
3. Peel and slice the onions. Crumble the bay leaves and thinly slice the well scrubbed lemon or the gherkins.
4. Fill the preserving jar with layers of herring, sliced onion, lightly crushed peppercorns, sliced lemon or gherkins and crumbled bay leaves.
5. Pour in enough vinegar to cover the contents of the jar, seal and marinade for at least a week before using.
6. Serve the pickled herrings on a bed of bean or alfalfa sprouts and garnish with parsley, lamb's lettuce or cress.

Tip:
The pickled herrings cannot be kept for more than 5-6 weeks, otherwise they will become too soft and will deteriorate in flavour.

Home pickled herrings are well worth the time and effort.

Poached cod

(Gepocheerde kabeljauw)

1 kg (2 lb) (2 pounds) fresh cod
4-5 peppercorns
salt
2 medium onions, sliced
1 leek, sliced
½ large carrot or a few small ones, roughly chopped
1 sprig thyme
1 bay leaf
small piece of mace
½ chopped stick celery
2 sprigs parsley
1 clove

1. Clean the fish if necessary. Scrub it well under cold running water, cut open the belly and remove the intestines, rinse well.
2. Place the fish in a suitable pan, cover it with cold water and add the lightly crushed peppercorns, salt to taste and the remaining ingredients. Bring the water to the boil, reduce the heat and simmer gently for approximately 9 minutes or until the flesh is white and can easily be removed from the bones.
3. Drain the cod well and serve on a warm plate with herb butter, melted butter, mustard or parsley sauce.

Tip:
Poach other types of fish in the same way, but adjust the cooking time. Smaller fish, such as whiting will be cooked in 3-4 minutes; more solid types of fish such as mullet or salmon will take up to 10 minutes depending on whether the fish is whole or cut into steaks.

Steamed mussels

(Gekookte mosselen)

2 kg (4 lb) (4 pounds) mussels
2 medium onions
2 medium leek
½ large carrot or 3 small ones
1 finely chopped stick celery
2-3 sprigs parsley
5 peppercorns
2-3 dl (7-10 fl oz) (⅞-1¼ cups) white wine

1. Scrub the mussels in plenty of cold running water. Cut away the beards and discard any mussels which are open or which feel unusually heavy – these may contain sand.
2. Peel and roughly chop the onion. Clean the leek and cut into pieces 5 cm (2 inches) long.
3. Scrape the carrot and cut into fairly large pieces. Wash the parsley. Put the chopped vegetables and herbs in a large heavy based pan, sprinkle in the lightly crushed peppercorns and fill the pan with the mussels.
4. Pour in the wine, cover the pan and bring the contents to the boil. Simmer gently for 8-9 minutes, shaking the pan occasionally, until all the mussels have opened.
5. Remove the pan from the heat and drain off the cooking liquid. Use this as a base for a sauce. Allow the mussels to cool for a few minutes and then remove them from their shells. Discard any which may have remained closed. Pile into a heated serving dish and serve with warm French bread and one of the sauces described below. The mussels can also be served in their shells – place a large empty dish on the table for the empty shells.

Tip:
A creamy onion, parsley or Béarnaise sauce is the ideal accompaniment to boiled or steamed mussels. Recipes for these can be found in the Sauce chapter on page 26. Use a little of the strained cooking liquid as a base for the sauce and season carefully.

Complete the menu by serving a clear soup as a starter and a mixed vegetable salad with the mussels.

Steamed mussels – a family meal with a continental flavour.

Stewed mussels from Zeeland

(Zeeuwse gestoofde mosselen)

500 g (1 lb) (1 pound) cooked mussels
1 dl (3½ fl oz) (½ cup) mussels stock
3-4 tbs (2-3 tbs) (2-3 tbs) cider or herb vinegar
60 g (2 oz) (¼ cup) butter
1 bay leaf or ½ tsp (¼ tsp) (¼ tsp) ground bay leaves
pinch ground nutmeg
1 onion or 2 shallots
2 Dutch rusks or 3 tbs (2 tbs) (2 tbs) dried breadcrumbs

1. Cook 1 kg (2 lb) (2 pounds) mussels as described in the previous recipe, remove them from the shells and weigh out 500 g (1 lb) (1 pound).
2. Melt the butter in a large heavy based pan and stir in the mussel stock and the vinegar. Add the bay leaf, a pinch of nutmeg and the peeled and finely chopped onion or shallots.
3. Crumble the rusks and stir into the pan. Spoon the mussels through the sauce, cover the pan and simmer gently for 45 minutes. Add a little extra mussel stock, white wine or water if necessary.
4. Serve with mashed potatoes and a crisp salad (iceberg lettuce, tomato, cucumber) with French dressing.

Baked dried cod with potatoes

(Stokvisschotel)

400-450 g (14-16 oz) (14-16 ounces) dried cod
1½ kg (3 lb) (3 pounds) potatoes
150-200 g (6-8 oz) (1-1⅓ cups) long grain rice
salt
700 g (¾ lb) (¾ pound) onions
80 g (3 oz) (6 tbs) butter
1½ tbs (1 tbs) (1 tbs) made mustard
2 tbs (1½ tbs) (1½ tbs) lightly soured cream
3 tbs (2 tbs) (2 tbs) dried breadcrumbs
1 tbs (½ tbs)(½ tbs) butter

1. Rinse the dried cod and soak for 2 days in several changes of cold water. Put the soaked and drained fish into a pan with just enough water to cover it.
2. Poach the dried cod for 40 minutes, drain and remove the skin and bones. Reserve a little of the cooking liquid for the sauce.
3. Peel the potatoes and cut them into small pieces. Wash the rice until the water runs clear.
4. Put the potatoes, fish and rice in a large heavy based pan with the drained cooking liquid and just enough water or light stock to cover the contents of the pan. Bring slowly to the boil.
5. Simmer gently for 40 minutes.
6. Peel and finely chop the onion. Melt the butter in a frying pan, 15 minutes before the end of the cooking time and sauté the onion until soft. Preheat the oven to 200 °C (400 °F).
7. Stir the mustard into the cream and spoon this through the fish and potatoes, together with the sautéed onion and pile the mixture into a lightly greased ovenproof dish.
8. Smooth the top with the back of a spoon, sprinkle with dried breadcrumbs and dot with flakes of butter. Bake until the top is golden brown and crispy. Serve hot.

Poached trout.

Poached trout

(Blauwgekookte forel)

approx. 4 dl (14 fl oz) (1¾ cups) vinegar
salt
5-6 peppercorns
2 sprigs parsley
1 finely chopped stick celery
2-3 small carrots
½ onion
1 clove
1 tsp (½ tsp) (½ tsp) grated lemon peel
4 fresh, cleaned rainbow trout, approx. 1 kg (2 lb)
(2 pounds) fish
125 g (4 oz) (½ cup) butter
1 lemon
3 tbs (2 tbs) (2 tbs) finely chopped chives

1. Rinse the trout carefully in cold running water –
take care not to damage the skin of the fish.
2. Curl the fish round and tie the head to the tail
with fine kitchen string.
3. Bring approximately 1½ l (2¾ pts) (6 cups) water
to the boil in a large pan and add the crushed peppercorns, parsley, celery, scraped and chopped carrots, peeled and chopped onion, clove and grated
lemon peel.
4. Heat the vinegar in a separate (non-aluminium)
pan to boiling point and fill a large pan with ice cold
water.
5. Dip the trout, one by one, into the simmering
vinegar and then plunge them immediately into the
pan with ice cold water. Leave for 15 minutes.
6. Transfer the fish to the pan of simmering water
and chopped vegetables and poach them for approximately 8 minutes, drain well, remove the
string and arrange on a heated serving dish.
7. Serve the blue trout (truite au bleu) with melted
butter, wedges of lemon and finely chopped chives.

Stewed eel with potatoes

(Zooitje)

1 kg (2 lb) (2 pounds) potatoes
500-600 g (1-1¼ lb) (1-1¼ pounds) cleaned eel
salt
freshly ground black pepper
2 tbs (1½ tbs) (1½ tbs) finely chopped parsley

for the sauce:
100 g (4 oz) (½ cup) butter
1 dl (3½ fl oz) (½ cup) wine or cider vinegar
½ tsp (¼ tsp) (¼ tsp) freshly ground black pepper
2 tsp (1½ tsp) (1½ tsp) cornflour, cornstarch or flour

1. Peel the potatoes, cut them into pieces and put them into a pan with 3 dl (½ pt) (1¼ cups) water.
2. Halve the eels if necessary and season with salt and freshly ground pepper. Pile them on top of the potatoes, cover the pan and simmer gently for approximately 20 minutes.
3. Drain off the cooking liquid, taking care that the pieces of eel remain whole and reserve the liquid for the sauce.
4. Arrange on a suitable serving dish and keep warm whilst preparing the sauce.
5. Melt the butter in a non-aluminium pan and stir in the eel stock and the vinegar.
6. Stir in the pepper and thicken the sauce with a cornflour blend. Pour the sauce over the fish and garnish with finely chopped parsley.

The Dutch Fishing Industry.
Many of the inhabitants of the small towns along the Dutch coast are fishermen by tradition. The reclamation of land during the past 50 years or so has had a considerable effect on the Dutch fishing industry, but many coastal towns still boast fine fleets of fishing boats. Nowadays all of these boats are fitted with powerful motors, so there are regular supplies of fresh fish to be had at the markets.
The Dutch fishing industry is very much based on salt water varieties – much of this is exported abroad.

Angling for fresh water fish is a much loved sport throughout Holland. An abundance of canals, rivers and small lakes provide ample opportunity for the amateur angler to practice his sport.

Aalsmeer fried eel

(Gebakken paling met stroop uit Aalsmeer)

600 g (1-1¼ lb) (1-1¼ pounds) cleaned fresh eel
salt
pinch freshly ground black pepper
1 tbs (½ tbs) (½ tbs) lemon juice
75 g (3 oz) (6 tbs) butter
4 tbs (3 tbs) (3 tbs) treacle or molasses
2 tbs (1½ tbs) (1½ tbs) cream

1. Rinse the eel in plenty of cold running water and cut into pieces, 6 cm (2½ inches) long. Arrange them upright in a shallow heavy based pan – pack them fairly tightly to ensure that they do not fall over during cooking.
2. Season with salt, freshly ground pepper and lemon juice and pour over 1 dl (3½ fl oz) (½ cup) water or fish stock. Cover the pan with a tightly fitting lid, bring to the boil and reduce the heat as soon as the liquid comes to the boil.
3. Remove the lid and allow the liquid to boil dry, taking care that the eel does not burn onto the base of the pan.
4. Melt the butter in a large heavy based frying pan and fry the pieces of eel, turning frequently to ensure even browning.
5. Heat the treacle or molasses in a small pan, stir in the cream and pour the hot sauce over the fried eel.
6. Serve warm or cold with fresh white toast.

Note:
This recipe originates from the small town of Aalsmeer, which is now no longer a fishing village due to the reclamation of land in that area. Most of the coastal towns and villages have their own recipes for eel, plaice and prawns – indeed, most of the people living along the coast have their own personal favourite recipes, ranging from very simple to haute cuisine. The idea of serving fried with a treacle sauce may sound a little strange, but many chefs use sweet ingredients such as fruit etc. to enhance the natural flavours of fish, meat and game. Not only does sugar add a certain subtlety to the flavour of the natural ingredients, it also makes the dish more substantial and often improves the texture of the main ingredient. The secret is to add not too much sweetening, otherwise the result will be sickly.

Deep fried smelts

(Gebakken spiering)

1 kg (2 lb) (2 pounds) or more, smelts
salt
freshly ground black pepper
5 dl (17 fl oz) (2 cups) milk
flour
oil or fat for deep frying

1. Clean the smelts by removing the heads and the intestines, rinse well in cold running water and season with salt and freshly ground pepper.
2. Drain the fish in a large colander and pat them dry with kitchen paper.
3. Dip them quickly into the milk and coat with flour.
4. Deep fry the smelts, a few at a time, drain and keep warm whilst the remainder are being cooked.

Tip:
Deep fried smelts are delicious as a cocktail or in-between snack. As part of a complete meal they can be served with fried potatoes, French fries or potato croquettes and a fresh mixed salad.

Fried sole

(Gebakken tong)

4 medium-sized, cleaned (Dover or lemon) sole
2-3 tbs (1-2 tbs) (1-2 tbs) lemon juice
salt
freshly ground black pepper
2 small eggs
1 tbs (½ tbs) (½ tbs) milk or thin cream
6 tbs (5 tbs) (5 tbs) dried breadcrumbs
125 g (4 oz) (½ cup) butter
4 slices lemon
finely chopped chives or parsley to garnish

1. Rinse the fish in cold running water, drain and pat dry with kitchen paper.
2. Rub the fish with a little lemon juice and season with salt and pepper to taste. Let them stand for 15-20 minutes before frying, to allow the flavour of the lemon juice to penetrate the fish.
3. Beat the eggs with the milk or thin cream and coat the sole, one by one, first with the beaten egg and then with the dried breadcrumbs.
4. Heat the butter in a large frying pan and fry the sole for approximately 2 minutes on each side, until they are golden brown and the flesh is cooked through. Fry no more than two at a time, otherwise the butter will cool off too quickly and the outside of the fish will not be crisp.
5. Serve the sole on warmed dinner plates or arrange on a large warm, flat dish and garnish with the slices of lemon. Sprinkle with a little finely chopped chives or parsley.

Tip:
Sole has a delicate flavour and tastes particularly good when served with creamed potatoes, duchesse potatoes, potato croquettes or simply with plain boiled rice, garnished with chopped parsley and Hollandaise sauce (see p. 29)

Sole fillet au gratin

(Gegratineerde tongfilets)

8 fillets of sole weighing approx. 1 kg
(2 lb) (2 pounds)
salt
50 g (2 oz) (4 tbs) butter
2 tbs (1 tbs) (1 tbs) grated cheese
2 tbs (1 tbs) (1 tbs) dried breadcrumbs
knob of butter

for the sauce:
40 g (1½ oz) (3 tbs) butter
30 g (1 oz) (3 tbs) flour
salt
5 dl (17 fl oz) (2 cups) milk
125 g (4 oz) (1⅓ cups) grated cheese
1 tbs (½ tbs) (½ tbs) tomato ketchup
½ tsp (¼ tsp) (¼ tsp) freshly ground black pepper

1. Rinse the fillets in cold running water and season with a little salt.
2. Melt the butter in a large frying pan and stew the fillets gently for about 8 minutes in the covered pan. They should be cooked through, but still remain whole. Meanwhile, prepare the cheese sauce.
3. Melt the butter in a heavy based pan and stir in the flour and salt to taste. Cook for 2-3 minutes, stirring all the time.
4. Heat the milk in a separate pan. Gradually add the milk, allowing the sauce to thicken and boil between each addition. When all the milk has been added, bring to the boil and simmer gently for about 5 minutes to make a smooth sauce.
5. Stir in the cheese and the tomato ketchup and continue stirring until the cheese has melted.
6. Season to taste with freshly ground pepper and pour half of the sauce into a warm, shallow ovenproof dish. Place the stewed fillets in the dish and cover with the remaining sauce.
7. Sprinkle over the dried breadcrumbs and grated cheese and dot with flakes of butter.
8. Place at the top of a hot oven (200°C) (400°F) and bake for approximately 10 minutes or until the top is crisp and golden brown.

Salmon parcels

(Zalm in aluminiumfolie)

*4 salmon steaks, approx. 175 g (6 oz) (6 ounces)
each
4 tbs (3 tbs) (3 tbs) lemon juice
salt
freshly ground black pepper
4 spring onions or scallions
2 small carrots
approx. 25 g (1 oz) (2 tbs) butter
2 limes or lemons
a few leaves of lamb's lettuce or iceberg lettuce*

1. Rinse the salmon steaks well, drain and pat dry
with kitchen paper. Dribble the lemon juice over
the fish and season with salt and freshly ground
pepper to taste.
2. Clean and trim the spring onions and separate
the shoots. Cut them into 8 cm (3 inches) lengths.
3. Scrape the carrots and cut into thin 8 cm (3
inches) strips.

4. Tear off 4 pieces of aluminium foil, 20 x 20 cm
(8 x 8 inches) square and place one salmon steak in
the centre of each piece. Cover with a few strips of
spring onion and carrot, add a small knob of butter
and pack tightly in the foil, taking care that the
edges are well sealed so that no steam can escape
during cooking. Place the salmon parcels in the top
half of a steamer.
5. Bring sufficient water to the boil in the bottom
half of the steamer and steam the fish for 20 minutes or until it is cooked through.
6. Serve the fish on a warm plate and garnish with a
slice of lime or lemon, a few washed lamb's lettuce
leaves or thin strips of iceberg lettuce. Small boiled
new potatoes are an excellent accompaniment to all
salmon dishes.

Tip:
Serve the salmon parcels with a chilled, dry white
wine – for example a Burgundy, Entre-deux-Mers
or Bordeaux. A light, fruity red wine would also be
a suitable accompaniment.

Salmon cooked in aluminium foil retains its fine flavour.

Meat

Braised top rib of beef

(Gebraden runderrollade)

serves 8

approx. 1 kg (2 lb) (2 pounds) rolled top rib of beef
salt, freshly ground pepper
125 g (4 oz) (½ cup) butter
1 bay leaf, 2 cloves
2 dl (7 fl oz) (⅞ cup) beef stock, fresh or from a
cube
2 tbs (1½ tbs) (1½ tbs) lightly soured cream

1. Rub the joint with salt and pepper and set aside
for 15 minutes.
2. Heat the butter in a large heavy based pan (with
lid) and wait until the foam has subsided. Brown
the joint of beef on all sides in the hot butter, approximately 10 minutes, and add the bay leaf and
cloves. Reduce the heat, cover the pan and braise
the beef for approximately 40 minutes, turning it
occasionally to ensure even cooking.
3. Remove the meat from the pan, keep it warm.
4. Stir the stock or water into the pan juices, scraping up the sediment at the bottom of the pan, boil
for a few minutes and then add the soured cream.
5. Remove the string from the beef, cut into fairly
thick slices and arrange on a warm serving plate.
6. Spoon a little of the sauce over the meat and
serve the rest separately.

Tip:
A thick roll of beef will require a slightly longer
cooking time than a long thin roll. Allow, on aver-
age, 20-30 minutes per 500 g (1 lb) (1 pound) of
meat, depending on how you like your beef
cooked. The cooking time given above will give a
medium rare result.

Note:
Most boned and rolled joints of meat sold in Holland are already seasoned with salt, pepper and
mixed spice. Unseasoned joints of meat have to be
ordered. If the joint is ready seasoned, then it will
not be necessary to rub it with salt and pepper before braising. The bay leaf and cloves, however,
add extra flavour to the gravy.

Braised marinaded beef

(Gestoofde gemarineerde runderlappen)

1½ dl (5 fl oz) (⅔ cup) beer or herb vinegar
1 tbs (½ tbs) (½ tbs) oil
1 large onion
2 bay leaves
2 cloves
salt
½ tsp (¼ tsp) (¼ tsp) freshly ground black pepper
pinch dried thyme
pinch dried basil
approx. 600 g (1¼ lb) (1¼ pounds) sliced stewing
beef
60 g (2 oz) (4 tbs) butter

1. Pour the beer, approximately 2 dl (7 fl oz)
(⅞ cup) water and the oil into a large dish.
2. Peel and slice the onion and add this to the beer,
together with the bay leaves, cloves, salt to taste,
pepper, thyme and basil. Stir well.
3. Immerse the stewing beef in the marinade, cover
with plastic film and refrigerate for at least 10 hours
before cooking, turning the meat occasionally.
4. Remove the meat from the marinade – reserve
this for the sauce. Pat the meat dry with kitchen paper.
5. Heat the butter in a large heavy based pan (with
lid) and brown the meat on all sides.
6. Strain the marinade, add this to the pan, cover
tightly and simmer very gently for approximately 2
hours or until the meat is really tender.

Tip:
Red or white cooking wine can be used instead of
beer. The acid in the wine or beer acts as a ten-
deriser.
Serve the marinaded beef with plain boiled rice,
pasta or potatoes.
This recipe also tastes good when served with
boerenkool or hutspot (see p. 76 and 82) instead of
smoked sausage or bacon.

Braised marinaded beef.

Dutch meatballs

(Gehaktballen)

500 g (1 lb) (1 pound) mince (half beef, half pork)
2 slices white bread
1 dl (3½ fl oz) (½ cup) milk
1 medium onion
1 small leek
1-2 small eggs
salt
freshly ground pepper
nutmeg
pinch curry powder or ground paprika
approx. 50 g (2 oz) (4 tbs) dried breadcrumbs
1½ tbs (1 tbs) (1 tbs) flour
100 g (4 oz) (½ cup) butter
1 dl (3½ fl oz) (½ cup) stock
2 tbs (1 tbs) (1 tbs) cream

1. Put the minced beef and pork into a large mixing bowl and loosen it with a fork.
2. Crumble the bread in a small basin and pour in the milk. Soak for a few minutes, squeeze it out and stir it into the mince.
3. Peel and finely chop the onion (and a clove of garlic if wished); clean and finely chop the leek and add them to the mince.
4. Lightly beat the eggs, season to taste with salt, pepper and a pinch of nutmeg and curry, add the dried breadcrumbs and stir into the mince.
5. Knead to combine all the ingredients – the mixture should not be too soft – and shape into 4 or 8 evenly sized meatballs.
Coat with a little flour.
6. Heat the butter in a large heavy based pan (with lid) and wait until the foam has subsided. Quickly brown the meatballs on all sides and remove them from the pan with a perforated spoon.
7. Stir the stock or water into the pan juices, scraping up the residue on the base of the pan, add the cream and return the meatballs to the pan.
8. Cover and simmer for approximately 20 minutes, turning the meatballs occasionally to ensure even cooking.

Minced steak patties

(Biefstuk tartaar)

approx. 400 g (14 oz) (14 ounces) minced steak
salt
freshly ground black pepper
pinch nutmeg
2 medium onions
1 egg yolk
2 tbs (1 tbs) (1 tbs) milk
flour
100 g (4 oz) (½ cup) butter
1 dl (3½ fl oz) (½ cup) beef stock
1 tbs (½ tbs)(½ tbs) cream

1. Put the minced steak into a bowl, season with salt, pepper and nutmeg and mix well.
2. Peel and finely chop one of the onions and thinly slice the other.
3. Lightly beat the egg yolk with the milk, stir in the chopped onion and knead this into the minced steak.
4. Shape into 4 evenly sized patties and coat with a little flour.
5. Heat the butter in a frying pan and wait until the foam has subsided; fry the patties quickly on both sides.
6. Reduce the heat, remove the patties from the pan and place on a warm, flat plate. Loosen the residue from the base of the pan with a wooden spoon and stir in the stock and the cream. Return the meat to the pan.
7. Warm the patties through in the sauce for 1-2 minutes, depending on how you like your beef cooked; and serve immediately.

Châteaubriand

(Gebakken dubbele biefstuk)

Serves 8

4 chateaubriand steaks
salt
freshly ground black pepper
approx. 100 g (4 oz) (½ cup) butter
1½ dl (5 fl oz) (⅔ cup) thin cream

1. Rub the steaks on both sides with salt and pepper.
2. Heat 50 g butter in a large frying pan and brown the meat quickly on both sides.
3. Add the remaining butter halfway through frying the steaks to ensure that the meat doesn't burn.
4. Remove the steaks from the pan – the cooking time will depend on how you like your beef cooked. Fry for 3 minutes longer on each side for medium rare steak.
5. Drain half of the butter out of the pan, stir in the cream and scrape up the residue on the base of the pan with a wooden spoon.
6. Slice the chateaubriands and serve on warm dinner plates, garnished with crisp green beans, courgette, cooked beetroot and strips of lettuce. Serve the sauce separately.

Note:
Chateaubriand steak is cut from the choicest part of the fillet and weighs approximately 250 g.

Tip:
Suitable vegetable accompaniments would be haricots verts, fresh asparagus, fresh mange-tout peas, artichoke hearts etcetera.
Serve with a full bodied red wine such as a Burgundy, Pomerol or Hermitage.

Châteaubriand.

Stewed beef with onions

(Hachee)

400-450 g (14-16 oz) (14-16 ounces) sliced brisket
salt
freshly ground black pepper
3 medium onions
80 g (3 oz) (6 tbs) butter
7 dl (1¼ pts) (3 cups) beef stock
2 cloves
2 bay leaves
approx. 5 peppercorns
3 tbs (2 tbs) (2 tbs) wine or herb vinegar
4 tbs (3 tbs) (3 tbs) flour, cornflour or cornstarch
2 tbs (1 tbs) (1 tbs) Indonesian sweet soya sauce or
an equal amount of soya sauce, sweetened with 2 tsp
(1 tsp)(1 tsp) sugar

1. Cut the brisket into small cubes, about 2 cm (1 inch) across. Season with salt and pepper and set aside whilst you prepare the onions.
2. Peel and finely chop the onions.
3. Heat the butter in a heavy based saucepan (with lid) and fry the onions gently for about 5 minutes.
4. Add the cubed meat and brown on all sides over a fairly high heat.
5. Stir in the (warm) stock, add the cloves, the bay leaves and lightly crushed peppercorns and then stir in the wine or vinegar.
6. Cover the pan and simmer the meat for 2-2½ hours or until it is tender.
7. Remove the bay leaves and the cloves, blend the flour with 4-5 tablespoons of cold water and use this to thicken the sauce.
8. Season with soya sauce to taste, adding the sugar if necessary.

Tip:
This recipe can also be made using cold leftover beef or pork. Sauté the chopped onion in 60 g (2 oz) (4 tbs) butter and stir in 60 g (2 oz) (6 tbs) flour. Add the stock to make a fairly thick sauce, stir in the chopped cold meat and complete the recipe as described above, 30-50 minutes should be sufficient to heat the meat through. Stir occasionally to prevent the sauce from sticking to the base of the pan.

Fried veal schnitzels

(Gebakken kalfsschnitzels)

4 veal schnitzels, approx. 100 g (4 oz) (4 ounces) each
salt
1 egg
2 tsp (1 tsp)(1 tsp) lemon juice
3 tbs (2 tbs) (2 tbs) flour
6 tbs (5 tbs) (5 tbs) dried breadcrumbs
approx. 125 g (4 oz) (½ cup) butter
4 slices lemon
4 anchovy fillets
capers to garnish

1. Place the schnitzels between 2 layers of non-stick baking paper and flatten them with a meat hammer or with the handle of a heavy knife. Set aside.
2. Beat the egg with a little lemon juice and coat the schnitzels with flour, then with beaten egg and finally with dried breadcrumbs.
3. Heat the butter in a large frying pan and wait until the foam has subsided. Fry the schnitzels for about 4 minutes on each side.
4. Arrange them on a warm serving plate, garnish each with a slice of lemon, a rolled up anchovy fillet and a few capers.

Tip:
Veal schnitzels also taste delicious when served with a simple cream sauce, or with Béarnaise or Béchamel sauce (see p. 27 and p. 28).

Veal birds

(Blinde vinken)

4 thin slices of lean veal, approx. 80 g (3 oz)
(3 ounces) each
salt
1 large egg
1 slice stale white bread,
100 g (4 oz) (4 ounces) veal mince
1 medium onion
1½ tsp (1 tsp) (1 tsp) freshly ground black pepper
ground allspice
ground nutmeg
1 egg white
2 tbs (1½ tbs) (1½ tbs) dried breadcrumbs
1 tbs (½ tbs)(½ tbs) lemon juice
125 g (4 oz) (½ cup) butter
4 slices lemon

1. Beat out the sliced veal as described in the previous recipe and season with a little salt. Set aside.
2. Beat the egg lightly, crumble the bread (crusts removed) and soak this in the egg.
3. Place the veal mince in a small basin and loosen it with a fork. Add the soaked bread and mix well.
4. Peel and finely chop the onion and stir it into the meat mixture, season with salt, pepper and a pinch each of allspice and nutmeg.
6. Divide the minced veal stuffing into 4 portions and place one on each slice of veal. Roll up and secure with wooden cocktail sticks or with thin kitchen string.
7. Lightly beat the egg white and coat the veal birds first with egg white and then with dried breadcrumbs.
8. Heat the butter in a large heavy based pan and wait until the foam has subsided. Brown the veal birds on all sides, glaze with a dash of stock or water and loosen the residue on the base of the pan with a wooden spoon. Stir in the lemon juice.
9. Simmer the veal birds for approximately 25 minutes or until the meat is tender, take them out of the pan and remove the cocktail sticks or string. Place on a warm serving dish.
10. Pour the gravy over the veal birds or serve separately and garnish with slices of lemon.

Variation:
Instead of coating the veal birds with egg and breadcrumbs you can wrap each in a thin slice of streaky bacon and then cook them as described above.

Tip:
Suitable accompaniments would be creamed potatoes, boiled new potatoes or a bowl of steaming boiled rice.

Braised sausages

(Gebakken, gestoofde saucijzen)

approx. 500 g (1 lb) (1 pound) coarse sausages
flour
60 g (2 oz) (4 tbs) butter
1 tbs (½ tbs) (½ tbs) tomato ketchup
a little thin cream
salt
freshly ground pepper

1. Place the sausages in a large pan and cover them with boiling water – leave for 30 seconds and then drain. This will help prevent the skins from bursting open during cooking.
2. Pat the sausages dry with kitchen paper and coat them with flour.
3. Heat the butter in a large heavy based frying pan (with lid) and wait until the foam has subsided. Brown the sausages quickly on all sides.
4. Add ½ dl (2 fl oz) (¼ cup) water or stock, mixed with the tomato ketchup and cream and loosen the residue on the base of the pan with a wooden spoon.
5. Cover the pan and simmer for 15-20 minutes, adding a little salt and pepper if necessary.
6. Serve the sausages on a warm plate and pour over the sauce or serve it separately.

Tip:
Serve with fried potatoes or a mixture of mashed potatoes and vegetables (on p. 77 e.g. Cabbage and potato mash). Home made apple sauce also tastes good with sausages.
Always take care when seasoning the accompanying sauce, as sausages are often quite highly seasoned in themselves.

Lamb cutlets with vegetable garnish

(Lamskoteletten met garnituur)

8 lamb cutlets
salt
freshly ground black pepper
ground allspice
ground nutmeg
150 g (6 oz) (2 cups) green beans
12 small carrots
150 g (6 oz) (6 ounces) broccoli
150 g (6 oz) (6 ounces) cauliflower
125-150 g (4-6 oz) (½ – ¾ cup) butter
4 tbs (3 tbs) (3 tbs) flour

1. Wipe the lamb cutlets with a damp cloth, pat them dry with kitchen paper and rub with salt, pepper and a pinch each of allspice and nutmeg. Set aside for 15 minutes.

2. Meanwhile, prepare the vegetables: wash the beans and cut into small pieces, scrape the carrots and wash the broccoli and cauliflower and divide into flowerets, reserving the stalks for soup or stock.

3. Steam the carrots for 7 minutes and the green beans, broccoli and cauliflower for 5 minutes. Keep warm.

4. Heat the butter in a large frying pan and wait until the foam has subsided. Coat the lamb cutlets with flour and cook four at a time. Brown in the hot butter, reduce the heat and cook gently for approximately 8 minutes on each side. Keep warm whilst the remainder are being cooked.

5. Arrange on a warm serving plate and garnish with the steamed vegetables. Serve with buttered new potatoes or creamy mashed potatoes.

Lamb cutlets with vegetable garnish.

Stewed lamb with mushrooms

(Lams-gies van de Veluwe)

400-450 g (14-16 oz) (14-16 ounces) lean lamb
flour
2 large onions
1 clove garlic
80-100 g (3-4 oz) (^{1}/₃ – ^{1}/₂ cup) butter
1 tbs (^{1}/₂ tbs) (^{1}/₂ tbs) finely chopped parsley
^{1}/₂ stalk finely chopped celery
2 tsp (1 tsp) (1 tsp) finely chopped mint
salt
freshly ground black pepper
pinch ground nutmeg
30 g (1 oz) (3 tbs) flour, cornflour or cornstarch
5 dl (17 fl oz) (2 cups) meat stock
approx. 100 g (4 oz) (4 ounces) button mushrooms
3 tbs (2 tbs) (2 tbs) cream or lightly soured cream

1. Cut the lamb into 2 cm (1 inch) cubes and coat them with a little flour.
2. Peel and chop the onion and garlic.
3. Heat half of the butter in a large heavy based pan and sauté the onion and garlic for about 5 minutes or until soft. Add the rest of the butter and raise the heat a little.
4. Stir in the cubed lamb and brown quickly on all sides.
5. Reduce the heat and add the finely chopped herbs, salt, pepper and nutmeg to taste. Mix well.
6. Stir in the flour and add the (warm) stock gradually, stirring continuously.
7. Cover the pan as soon as the sauce has thickened and simmer very gently for approximately 1½ hours or until the meat is tender. Stir occasionally and add a little extra stock or water if necessary.
8. Add the cleaned and halved or quartered mushrooms approximately 12 minutes before the end of the cooking time.
9. Remove the pan from the heat and stir in the cream.

Tip:
Serve with warm wholemeal or granary bread, or with brown French bread, a mixture of stewed pears and stewed prunes and steamed leeks, endive or cabbage. Traditionally one should drink a glass of buttermilk with this dish!

Note:
This is an old recipe from the Veluwe, a richly forested area in the east of Holland. The story goes that as two tramps were passing a farmhouse they smelt the delicious aroma of a rich meat stew. As they had not eaten for several days, they hatched a plan for stealing the food. They decided that one of them, called Ies, should call out "the bull has escaped" and that the other, called Gies, would then creep into the kitchen during the general panic and steal the pan of stew. This plan succeeded but the two vagabonds ate so much food that they fell into a deep sleep, clutching the empty pot between them. The farmer's wife, by now furious, caught them in their reverie and beat them with the cooking pot. They fled off into the night and never returned. Since then all types of stewed meat in this area have been nicknamed Ies en Gies is Pannegies (Ies and Gies is Panniegies) or simply Pannegies for short.

Jugged hare

(Hazepeper)

1 hare
salt
1 tsp (½ tsp) (½ tsp) freshly ground black pepper
pinch thyme
pinch oregano
1 medium onion
60 g (2 oz) (4 tbs) butter
4 tbs (3 tbs) (3 tbs) sunflower oil
2 tsp (1 tsp) (1 tsp) coarse mustard
2 tsp (1 tsp) (1 tsp) sugar
40 g (1½ oz) (4 tbs) flour
1 dl (3½ fl oz) (½ cup) lightly soured cream

for the marinade:
4 dl (14 fl oz) (1¾ cups) red wine
1 dl (3½ fl oz) (½ cup) water
1 tbs (½ tbs) (½ tbs) wine vinegar
1 tbs (½ tbs) (½ tbs) tomato ketchup
2 onions
2 bay leaves
5-6 black peppercorns

1. Joint the hare, wipe clean and rub with a mixture of salt, pepper, thyme and oregano. Set aside and prepare the marinade.
2. Pour the red wine, water and vinegar into a large dish and stir in the tomato ketchup. Peel and roughly chop the onions and add them to the wine mixture, together with the crumbled bay leaves and crushed peppercorns.
3. Put the jointed hare into the marinade, cover the dish with plastic film and refrigerate overnight.
4. The next day, remove the hare from the marinade, pat dry with kitchen paper and strain the marinade for the sauce.
5. Heat the butter and oil in a large heavy based pan and brown the joints of hare on all sides.
6. Stir the mustard and the sugar into the sieved marinade and pour it into the pan. Bring to the boil, cover the pan, reduce the heat and simmer gently for approximately 2½ hours or until the hare is tender.
7. Use a draining spoon to remove the meat from the pan, arrange the pieces on a heated dish and

keep them warm.
8. Blend the flour with a little water, stock or wine and use it to thicken the cooking liquid.
9. Remove the pan from the heat, stir in the cream and pour a little of the sauce over the hare. Serve the rest separately.

Tip:
Serve the jugged hare with home made apple, peach or apricot sauce, or with a spicy cranberry compote.
Suitable vegetable accompaniments would be boiled or creamed potatoes or plain boiled rice and a crisp green salad.

Rabbit in cream sauce

(Konijn met roomsaus)

1 wild rabbit
salt
freshly ground pepper
pinch thyme
pinch ground bay leaves
100 g (4 oz) (½ cup) butter
1 dl (3½ fl oz) (½ cup) red wine
1 dl (3½ fl oz) (½ cup) meat or chicken stock
1 tbs (½ tbs) (½ tbs) lemon juice
1 tbs (½ tbs) (½ tbs) tomato paste
2 tbs (1 tbs) (1 tbs) arrowroot or potato flour
1 dl (3½ fl oz) (½ cup) thin cream

1. Joint the rabbit and wipe the pieces clean. Rub them with a mixture of salt, pepper, thyme and bay leaves.
2. Heat the butter in a large heavy based pan and wait until the foam subsides. Brown the rabbit on all sides.
3. Reduce the heat and add the wine, stock, lemon juice and tomato paste, stir well, cover the pan and simmer gently for at least 2 hours or until the rabbit is tender.
4. Remove the meat from the pan, arrange the pieces on a suitable serving dish and keep them warm.
5. Blend the arrowroot with 3 spoonfuls of water and use this to thicken the sauce. Cook gently for

2 minutes, stirring all the time.
6. Pour the sauce over the stewed rabbit and serve immediately.

Tip:
Serve with boiled or creamed potatoes or with plain boiled rice and a tangy fruit sauce, apple and apricot for example. A light, sparkling wine would be the ideal wine to drink with this dish.

Variation:
Use a small domestic rabbit, instead of the wild variety. Domestic rabbits are usually larger than wild ones.

Saddle of venison with cranberry sauce

(Reerug met vossebessensaus)

serves approx. 12

1 saddle of venison, weighing approx. 2½ kg (5 lb) (5 pounds)
salt
freshly ground pepper
250 g (8 oz) (1 cup) butter
1 dl (3½ fl oz) (½ cup) white wine
1 dl (3½ fl oz) (½ cup) light stock
2 dl (7 fl oz) (⅞ cup) lightly soured cream
4-5 tbs (3-4 tbs) (3-4 tbs) cranberry jelly

for the marinade:
3 dl (½ pt) (1¼ cups) red wine
2 dl (7 fl oz) (⅞ cup) herb vinegar
½ dl (2 fl oz) (¼ cup) water
3 tbs (2 tbs) (2 tbs) olive or sunflower oil
salt
6 black peppercorns
pinch ground thyme
pinch ground bay leaves or 2 whole bay leaves

1. Wipe the meat and rub with salt and pepper. Set aside and prepare the marinade.
2. Pour the wine, vinegar, water and oil into a large dish and add the salt, crushed peppercorns, thyme and bay leaves. Stir well. Put the venison into the marinade, cover the dish with plastic film and marinade for 12-24 hours in a cool place.
3. Remove the meat from the marinade, pat it dry and melt the butter in a large heavy based pan. Wait until the butter starts to turn golden brown and then brown the meat on all sides. Add the (warmed) wine and stock and scrape up the residue from the base of the pan with a wooden spoon.
4. Cover the pan and simmer gently for 1½ – 2 hours until the venison is tender.
5. Remove the meat from the pan and carefully cut away the bones. Carve the meat in fairly thick slices and arrange them on a heated serving dish in their original form.
6. Stir the cream and the cranberry jelly into the sauce, heat gently for no more than 2 minutes and pour a little over the meat. Serve the remaining sauce separately.

Tip:
Serve the venison in the centre of a large flat meat plate and pipe small rosettes of chestnut puree around the edge. Potato croquettes, game chips and sprouts or chicory wrapped in ham would be suitable vegetable accompaniments.

Chestnut puree and cranberry jelly are both readily available in tins and jars respectively.

Variation:
Use an equal amount of strained marinade instead of the red wine and stock for a piquanter sauce.

Braised chicken roll

(Gebraden kuikenrollade)

serves approx. 6

1 large or 12 individual rolled chicken joints,
approx. 750 g (1½ lb) (1½ pounds) total weight
salt
freshly ground pepper
150 g (6 oz) (¾ cup) butter
1 dl (3½ fl oz) (½ cup) dry white wine
1 dl (3½ fl oz) (½ cup) meat or chicken stock
pinch ground ginger
pinch thyme
pinch rosemary
1 tbs (½ tbs) (½ tbs) cornflour, cornstarch or flour
1-2 tsp (½ – 1 tsp) (½ – 1 tsp) sugar
3 drops Worcestershire sauce
1 tbs (½ tbs) (½ tbs) tomato paste

1. Rub the rolled chicken with salt and pepper to taste.
2. Heat the butter in a large heavy based pan, wait until the foam subsides and brown the meat on all sides.
3. Reduce the heat and add the white wine, stock and herbs. Scrape up the residue from the base of the pan with a wooden spoon.
4. Cover the pan and simmer gently for about 50 minutes for the large joint or 20 minutes for the individual ones or until the chicken is tender. Turn the joint regularly to ensure that it cooks evenly.
5. Remove the chicken from the pan, cut away the string and slice fairly thickly. Arrange the slices on a serving dish. Leave individual joints whole.
6. Strain the cooking liquid into a small pan, blend the cornflour with 1-2 tablespoons of cold water and use this to thicken the sauce.
7. Pour a little of the sauce over the meat and serve the rest separately.

Tip:
Suitable vegetable accompaniments would be sprouts, cabbage leaves stuffed with rice, koolrabi or broccoli. Decorate the serving dish with a few piped rosettes of creamed potato.

Individual braised chicken rolls.

Fried chicken livers

(Gebakken kippelever)

500 g (1 lb) (1 pound) chicken livers
1 tbs (½ tbs) (½ tbs) flour
2 medium onions
1 clove garlic
1 small leek
75 g (3 oz) (6 tbs) butter
100 g (4 oz) (4 ounces) button mushrooms
1 green or red pepper
1 dl (3½ fl oz) (½ cup) red or white wine
1 dl (3½ fl oz) (½ cup) chicken stock
1½ tbs (1 tbs) (1 tbs) cornflour or cornstarch
salt
pepper
1 tsp (½ tsp) (½ tsp) ready made mild mustard
2 tbs (1 tbs) (1 tbs) Madeira
1 tsp (½ tsp) (½ tsp) chilli sauce

1. Rinse the chicken livers in cold, running water, remove any membranes and drain in a sieve. Toss them in the flour.
2. Peel and finely chop the onions and the garlic.
3. Wash the leek and slice into thin rings.
4. Heat the butter in a large heavy based pan and wait until the foam has subsided. Sauté the onion, garlic and leek until soft.
5. Add the chicken livers and turn them in the hot butter until they are light golden brown.
6. Meanwhile, wipe the mushrooms, trim the base of the stalks and cut them in half. Add them to the chicken livers and sauté for a few minutes.
7. Halve the pepper, remove the seeds and white pith and chop the flesh into cubes or slice thinly. Stir them into the chicken liver mixture and sauté for 3 minutes.
8. Add the wine and stock and bring the contents of the pan to the boil. Blend the cornflour with 1-2 tablespoons of cold water and use this to thicken the pan juices.
9. Season to taste with salt and pepper and stir in the mustard, Madeira and chilli sauce. Simmer gently for 10-12 minutes and serve hot.

Tip:
Fried chicken livers taste delicious with plain boiled rice or creamed potatoes. Chilled white wine would be a suitable accompaniment.

Braised stuffed chicken

(Gevulde kip)

1 roasting chicken
200 g (7 oz) (7 ounces) minced veal or a mixture of minced beef and pork
1 medium onion
1 small leek
1 slice stale bread, crusts removed
1 egg
salt
freshly ground pepper
pinch ground nutmeg
pinch ground paprika or curry powder
2 tbs (1½ tbs) (1½ tbs) finely chopped parsley or chives
75 g (3 oz) (6 tbs) butter
1-1½ dl (3½ – 5 fl oz) (½ – ⅔ cup) stock

1. Wipe the chicken with a damp cloth and pat dry with kitchen paper.
2. Put the mince into a bowl. Peel and finely chop the onion, wash and finely chop the leek, crumble the bread and work these ingredients into the mince.
3. Lightly beat the egg and season to taste with salt, pepper, nutmeg, paprika and the chopped parsley. Work the seasoned egg into the minced meat and use this to stuff the chicken.
4. Sew up the neck or secure the loose skin with wooden cocktail sticks. Melt the butter in a large heavy based pan; brown the chicken on all sides.
5. Reduce the heat, pour the stock into the pan and scrape up the residue on the base of the pan with a wooden spoon. Cover and simmer gently for 1 hour, turning the chicken occasionally to ensure even cooking.
6. Remove the chicken from the pan and carve at the table.
7. Add a dash of cream to the sauce or serve it as it is.

Sliced turkey breast with chive sauce, served with a colourful vegetable garnish – a delicious meal.

Turkey breast with chive sauce

(Kalkoenfilet met bieslooksaus)

2-3 small turkey breasts, total weight 600 g (1¼ lb)
(1¼ pounds)
2 tbs (1½ tbs) (1½ tbs) flour
salt
freshly ground black pepper
pinch rosemary
pinch basil
150 g (6 oz) (¾ cup) butter
Hollandaise sauce (p. 29)
3 tbs (2 tbs) (2 tbs) finely chopped chives

1. Coat the turkey breasts with flour seasoned with a little salt, pepper and a pinch each of rosemary and basil.
2. Heat the butter in a large heavy based pan or frying pan and wait until the foam has subsided. Fry the turkey breasts for about 5 minutes on each side or until cooked through and golden brown.
3. Remove them from the pan and carve into slices 1 cm (½ inch) thick. Arrange these on warm dinner plates and keep warm.
4. Prepare a vegetable garnish of lightly cooked cauliflower, mange-tout peas, steamed sweetcorn, fried sliced aubergine and steamed carrot sticks.
5. Serve with warm Hollandaise sauce (p. 29) and sprinkle with finely chopped chives.

Braised wild duck

(Gebraden eend)

2 small, ready to cook wild duck
salt
freshly ground pepper
100 g (4 oz) (½ cup) butter
approx. 1½ dl (5 fl oz) (⅔ cup) light stock or white
wine

1. Rinse the ducks briefly under cold running water, pat them dry with kitchen paper and rub them with salt and pepper. A little thyme or rosemary can also be used to season the ducks.
2. Heat the butter in a large heavy based pan and brown the ducks quickly on all sides once the foam has subsided.
3. Add the stock, cover the pan, bring to the boil, reduce the heat once the stock is boiling and simmer gently for about 1 hour or until the ducks are tender. Turn them occasionally to ensure even cooking.
4. Remove the birds from the pan, add a little extra stock or wine to the sauce and serve separately. Carve the ducks at the table.

Tip:
Garnish the serving plate with slices of orange, marinaded in a little orange liqueur and garnish each with a glacé cherry.
Serve with a seasonal salad or with steamed green beans, broccoli or cauliflower.

Variation:
Use domestic duck if wild duck is not available. Use 1 large duck or 2 small ducklings and cook for the time recommended by your poultry dealer. Wild duck tends to be more popular in Holland than the domestic variety.

Pheasant with sauerkraut

(Fazant met zuurkool)

100 g (4 oz) (4 ounces) sliced lean streaky bacon
approx. 750 g (1½ lb) (1½ pounds) sauerkraut,
matured in white wine
1 medium onion or 3 shallots
1 eating apple, e.g. James Grieve or Golden
Delicious
6 black peppercorns, 6 juniper berries
2 dl (7 fl oz) (⅞ cup) white wine
1 dl (3½ fl oz) (½ cup) light stock
2 medium potatoes, peeled and grated
1 pheasant
salt, freshly ground black pepper
pinch ground bay leaves, pinch ground nutmeg
100 g (4 oz) (½ cup) butter

1. Line the base of a suitable heavy based pan with the sliced bacon.
2. Loosen the strands of sauerkraut with two forks and spread this over the bacon.
3. Peel and finely chop the onion and the cored apple and pile them onto the sauerkraut, together with the lightly crushed peppercorns and juniper berries.
4. Pour in the wine and the stock, cover the pan and bring the contents slowly to the boil.
5. Reduce the heat and simmer gently for approximately 30 minutes. Meanwhile, rub the pheasant with salt and pepper to taste and a pinch each of ground bay leaves and nutmeg and set aside.
6. Heat the butter in a large heavy based pan, wait until the foam has subsided and brown the pheasant on all sides. Cover the pan and braise the pheasant over a low heat, turning occasionally to ensure even cooking.
7. Stir the grated potatoes into the sauerkraut and place the pheasant on top. Simmer gently for approximately 1 hour or until the pheasant is cooked through, adding a little extra wine or stock if necessary to prevent the sauerkraut from drying out.

Tip:
Serve with røsti, creamed potatoes or potato croquettes and a fruity red wine, for example a Bordeaux or Beaujolais.

Dutch apple sauce

(Appelmoes)

1½ kg (3 lb) (3 pounds) cooking apples
1 stick cinnamon
125 g (4 oz) (½ cup) sugar
3 tbs (2 tbs) (2 tbs) lemon juice

1. Peel and quarter the apples, remove the cores and put them into a large pan.
2. Pour in approximately 2 dl (7 fl oz) (⅞ cup) water, tuck the stick of cinnamon under the apples and cook for approximately 10 minutes or until the apples are soft and pulpy. Stir occasionally to prevent the apples from sticking to the base of the pan.
3. Remove the pan from the heat, take out the cinnamon and beat the apples into a smooth pulp with a wooden spoon. Add the sugar and stir until dissolved.
4. Sharpen the sauce with the lemon juice and serve warm or cold.

Variation:
Flavour the apple sauce with lemon instead of with cinnamon. Scrub a lemon, peel as thinly as possible and tuck the lemon peel under the apples before cooking. Sprinkle a little ground cinnamon over the apple sauce just before serving.
Sweeten the sauce with honey or brown sugar instead of with white sugar. The flavour of the honey is determined by the type of flower from which the nectar has been collected. Honey made from clover nectar tastes particularly good with apple sauce as does the clear, deep yellow fragrant honey made from heather nectar and the clear amber honey, made from a mixture of different types of flowers. Buckwheat honey has a fairly strong flavour which tends to mask the delicate flavour of the apples.

Note:
Fruit sauces or compotes are often served as a vegetable course in Holland.

Rhubarb compote

(Rabarbercompote)

1 kg (2 lb) (2 pounds) rhubarb
4 tbs (3 tbs) (3 tbs) lemon juice
approx. 175 g (6 oz) (¾ cup) sugar
1 tbs (½ tbs) (½ tbs) cornflour or cornstarch
2 tbs (1 tbs) (1 tbs) white wine
pinch ground cinnamon

1. Remove the leaves and trim the stalks of the rhubarb. Wash well and slice into pieces, 3 cm (1½ inches) long.
2. Put the rhubarb into a large pan, add approximately 3 dl (½ pt)(1¼ cups) water and the lemon juice. Bring slowly to the boil.
3. Add the sugar as the water comes to the boil, cover and simmer gently for 7-8 minutes or until the rhubarb is soft.
4. Arrange the rhubarb with a perforated spoon into a serving dish and blend the cornflour with the wine.
5. Thicken the juice with the cornflour blend and boil for 1 minute.
6. Pour the sauce over the rhubarb and dust the top with a little ground cinnamon.

Stewed pears

(Stoofperen)

1½ kg (3 lb) (3 pounds) stewing pears
approx. 60 g (2 oz) (¼ cup) sugar
1 stick of cinnamon or the peel from 1 lemon
1 tbs (½ tbs) (½ tbs) cornflour, cornstarch,
arrowroot or potato flour

1. Peel and quarter or halve the pears, remove the cores and put them into a large pan.
2. Pour in approximately 4 dl (14 fl oz) (1¾ cups) water, add the sugar, cinnamon or lemon peel and bring to the boil.
3. Reduce the heat as soon as the water comes to the boil, cover and simmer for approximately 1 hour or until the pears are soft and deep red in colour (this will depend on the variety of the pear – the Dutch always use a variety called Gieser Wilderman which turn deep red when cooked). Add a little extra water or red wine if the cooking liquid evaporates before the pears are soft.
4. Remove the cinnamon or lemon peel and transfer the pears to a large fruit bowl, using a perforated spoon.
5. Blend the cornflour with 1-2 spoonfuls of cold water and use this to thicken the pear juice. Pour the sauce over the pears and serve hot or cold.

Tip:
Replace 1 dl (3½ fl oz) (½ cup) of the water with blackcurrant juice if the red variety of cooking pear is not available.

Variation:
Replace a few of the pears with dried or fresh apricots and sweeten the juice with 5-6 spoonfuls of honey instead of with sugar.

Baked chicory

(Gegratineerde witlof)

1 kg (2 lb) (2 pounds) chicory
salt
dried breadcrumbs
25 g (1 oz) (2 tbs) butter
ground nutmeg

1. Remove the outside leaves of the chicory and cut a cone-shaped piece out of the base of the stalk – this has a bitter taste. Wash them and put into a large pan. Cover with cold water and season with salt to taste.
2. Bring the chicory to the boil and simmer gently for approximately 15 minutes. Drain well in a colander. Reserve 1 dl (3½ fl oz) (½ cup) of the liquid for the sauce.
3. Preheat the oven to 200 °C (400 °F), grease an ovenproof dish with a little oil or butter, arrange the drained chicory in the dish and pour over the reserved cooking liquid.
4. Sprinkle with the breadcrumbs, dot with flakes of butter and bake for approximately 20 minutes until the surface is golden brown.
5. Dust with a little ground nutmeg and serve with boiled or creamed potatoes.

Tip:
For a simple meal, butter a second ovenproof dish and fill with frozen røsti or grated par-boiled potatoes. Sprinkle with salt and pepper, dot with flakes of butter and bake alongside the chicory in the oven.

Variation:
Leeks can be served in the same manner – the cooking and baking times are the same as for the chicory.

Swede with white sauce

(Koolraap met bloemsaus)

1 kg (2 lb) (2 pounds) swede
salt
1 tsp (½ tsp)(½ tsp)sugar
30 g (1 oz) (2 tbs) butter
30 g (1 oz) (3 tbs) flour
2 dl (7 fl oz) (⅞ cup) milk
freshly ground pepper
pinch ground nutmeg
½ tsp (¼ tsp) (¼ tsp) curry powder

1. Peel the swede and cut into slices 1½ cm (¾ inch) thick. Cut the slices into sticks or cubes, rinse well and bring to the boil in a large pan with a little water and salt and sugar to taste.
2. Simmer gently for about 15 minutes or until the swede is tender, drain and reserve approximately 1 dl (3½ fl oz) (½ cup) of the cooking liquid for the sauce. Keep the swede warm.
3. Melt the butter in a small pan and stir in the flour. Cook for 2-3 minutes, stirring continuously. Gradually add the milk and the cooking liquid to make a smooth thick sauce and simmer gently for about 3 minutes.
4. Add salt and pepper to taste and season with a pinch of ground nutmeg and the curry powder.
5. Pour the sauce over the swede and serve immediately.

Boiled escarole

(Gekookte andijvie)

1½ kg (3 lb) (3 pounds) escarole or curly endive
salt
30 g (1 oz) (2 tbs) butter
approx. 20 g (¾ oz) (2 tbs) cornflour or cornstarch
1 dl (3½ fl oz) (½ cup) milk or light stock
pinch ground nutmeg

1. Wash the escarole thoroughly and remove any brown or damaged leaves.
2. Shred the leaves and pile them into a large pan.
3. Add a small amount of water and a little salt and bring to the boil. Cook gently for about 12 minutes – turn the escarole after 5 minutes to ensure that the top layer comes in contact with the heat at the bottom of the pan.
4. Drain and reserve 1 dl (3½ fl oz) (½ cup) of the cooking liquid for the sauce.
5. Stir the butter into the warm liquid, add the milk or stock and blend the cornflour with a little cold water. Thicken the sauce with the cornflour blend and cook for 1 minute, stirring all the time.
6. Spoon the cooked escarole through the sauce and sprinkle with a little ground nutmeg.

Variation:
If you prefer not to use a sauce, simply shake a couple of spoonfuls of butter through the cooked escarole and sprinkle in some dried breadcrumbs to absorb any excess moisture. The cooked and drained escarole can also be stirred into 2 dl (7 fl oz) (⅞ cup) creamy Béchamel sauce (see p. 27). Spoon a little grated cheese or some thinly sliced ham into the cooked escarole and serve with pan or French fried potatoes.

Note:
Most Dutch greengrocers serve a variety of ready chopped raw vegetables which simply need to be rinsed and then cooked.

Savoury leek tartlets

(Preitaartjes)

See photo on p. 72-73.

for the pastry:
50 g (2 oz) (4 tbs) cold butter
100 g (4 oz)(¾ cup) flour
salt
1 egg yolk
½ dl (2 fl oz) (¼ cup) cold water
butter or margarine
for the filling:
2 shallots or spring onions or scallions
4 small leeks
25 g (1 oz) (2 tbs) butter
100 g (4 oz) (4 ounces) sliced streaky bacon
freshly ground black pepper
100 g (4 oz) (1⅓ cups) grated mature cheese

1. Rub the fat into the flour and salt until it resembles fine breadcrumbs and mix with the egg yolk and the cold water to make a firm dough.
2. Dust the working surface with flour and roll out the dough to a thickness of 3 mm (¹⁄₁₆ inch).
3. Lightly grease 4 individual flan cases and line them with the pastry. Trim away any excess dough.
4. Peel and chop the shallots; wash the leeks, remove any coarse leaves and cut into thin strips. Preheat the oven to 200°C (400°F).
5. Melt the butter in a frying pan and sauté the shallots until they are soft. Add the bacon and the strips of leek and sauté for a further 2-3 minutes. Dust with a little freshly ground black pepper.
6. Roll up the bacon and divide the rolls between the lined flan cases. Arrange the leeks on top of the bacon and cover with grated cheese. Season with a little salt if necessary, but take care the bacon and the cheese already contain fair amounts of salt.
7. Place the tartlets on a baking sheet and bake for 15-25 minutes or until the tops are golden brown. Serve as a hot starter or as an in-between snack.

Boiled fennel

(Venkel met saus)

approx. 1 kg (2 lb) (2 pounds) fennel
salt
1 tbs (½ tbs) (½ tbs) cornflour or cornstarch
25 g (1 oz) (2 tbs) butter

1. Wash the fennel, trim the soft fronds, slice off the bases and remove any damaged or brown outside leaves. Cut each into quarters or slice fairly thickly.
2. Put the fennel in a pan with approximately 1½ dl (5 fl oz) (⅔ cup) boiling water and a little salt to taste. Bring the contents of the pan back to the boil, cover and simmer gently for about 18 minutes or until the fennel is tender but still firm to the bite. The pieces should retain their shape.
3. Drain and spoon into a warm serving dish – reserve the liquid for the sauce.
4. Blend the cornflour with a couple of spoonfuls of water or stock and use this blend to thicken the reserved cooking liquid.
5. Stir the butter into the sauce and spoon it over the fennel.

Variation:
Kohlrabi or celeriac can also be prepared in the same way. Check the vegetables after 15 minutes – they may require less cooking time than the fennel.

Tip:
This fragrant vegetable tastes delicious as an accompaniment to lamb or veal. Serve with creamed potato or small buttered new potatoes. Boiled or braised fennel can also be served with savoury meatballs or grilled pork chops.

On following pages: Leek tartlets – an attractive warm starter.

Chopped spinach

(Gekookte spinazie)

2 kg (4 lb) (4 pounds) fresh spinach
2 eggs
50 g (2 oz) (4 tbs) butter
salt
3 tbs (2 tbs) (2 tbs) dried breadcrumbs
2 slices stale white bread

1. Wash the spinach in plenty of cold water, drain and pile into a large saucepan. Bring the contents of the pan slowly to the boil and turn the spinach several times to ensure that the top layer also cooks through.
2. Reduce the heat and simmer gently for about 8 minutes, or until the spinach is soft, stirring occasionally. Meanwhile, hard boil the eggs, plunge them into cold water, remove the shells and cut into wedges or slices.
3. Drain the spinach in a sieve, pressing it well down to remove as much of the liquid as possible. Chop finely with a large sharp knife. Heat half of the butter in a heavy based pan and add the chopped spinach. Season with salt to taste and thicken with the dried breadcrumbs – these will absorb any excess liquid still remaining. Pile the cooked spinach into a heated dish and keep it warm.
4. Remove the crusts from the bread, cut each slice into thin strips or cubes and fry them golden brown in the remaining butter.
5. Garnish the spinach with fried bread and wedges or slices of egg.

Steamed purslane

(Gekookte postelein)

1½ kg (3 lb) (3 pounds) purslane
salt
30 g (1 oz) (2 tbs) butter
1 tbs (½ tbs) (½ tbs) arrowroot or potato flour

1. Wash the purslane in plenty of cold water, remove any damaged leaves and trim away the roots. Drain and roughly chop the leaves.
2. Pile the purslane into a large pan and bring slowly to the boil. Turn the purslane to ensure that the top layer comes in contact with the heat at the bottom of the pan. Reduce the heat and simmer gently for about 10 minutes, stirring occasionally.
3. Drain if necessary and reserve a little of the cooking liquid for the sauce.
4. Blend the arrowroot with a couple of spoonfuls of water or stock and use this to thicken the sauce. Season with salt, stir in the butter and spoon the drained purslane through the sauce. Serve with creamed potatoes or small boiled new potatoes.

Note:
Purslane is very popular in Holland, but may be less available in England or in the United States. It is similar to spinach and escarole and shrinks dramatically in volume during cooking, due to the high water content. Allow at least 350 g (12 oz) (12 ounces) raw purslane per person. It can be kept for 2-3 days in an open plastic bag in the vegetable compartment of the refrigerator.

Tip:
The sauce can also be thickened with lightly beaten egg instead of with arrowroot if preferred.

Variation:
Young turnip tops can also be cooked in the same way. These are readily available in Holland during the late winter months (February) and are usually sold in bundles weighing about 200 g (8 oz) (8 ounces). Serve with a simple sauce, as described above, or with a white sauce as described on p. 70 (Swede with white sauce).

Creamed potatoes

(Aardappelpuree)

1½ kg (3 lb) (3 pounds) floury potatoes
salt
approx. 3 dl (½ pt) (1¼ cups) warm milk
40 g (1½ oz) (3 tbs) or more butter
1-2 egg yolks
grated nutmeg

1. Peel the potatoes or scrub the skins and boil them for approximately 20 minutes or until cooked through. Drain, peel potatoes boiled in their skins and put them into a large mixing bowl.
2. Add salt to taste, the milk, butter, cut into pieces, and the lightly beaten egg yolks and beat well to make a smooth, light puree. The best way to do this is with an electric hand mixer.
3. Dust with a little grated nutmeg and serve immediately.

Note:
The Dutch are very fond of floury potatoes, so most varieties cultivated in Holland tend to be of this type. The best way to cook floury potatoes is to steam them in a steamer or boil fast in very little water so that they do not have time to become mushy. Drain off any excess water, return the potatoes to the pan and dry them over a low heat, shaking the pan from time to time to prevent the potatoes from burning.

Variation:
Pile the creamed potatoes into a lightly greased ovenproof dish. Preheat the oven to 160 °C (325 °F), sprinkle a layer of dried breadcrumbs over the potatoes and dot with flakes of butter. Bake in the centre of the oven for about 25 minutes or until the top is crisp and golden brown.

Stuffed cabbage leaves

(Gevulde koolrolletjes)

1½ kg (3 lb) (3 pounds) green or chinese cabbage
400-500 g (12-16 oz) (12-16 ounces) minced beef or beef and pork mixed
1 egg yolk
pinch mixed herbs
leftover gravy
50 g (2 oz) (4 tbs) butter
2-3 tbs dried breadcrumbs
1-2 tbs (½-1 tbs)(½-1 tbs) butter or stock

1. Wash the cabbage and separate the leaves. Steam them in a little salted water until they are cooked through, but not too soft. Drain well.
2. Put the minced meat into a bowl and mix in the beaten egg, herbs, salt and pepper to taste. Shape them into small sausage shaped rolls, about 4 cm (1 ½ inches) thick, and 8 cm (3 inches) long.
3. Heat the butter in a heavy based frying pan and brown the rolls of mince on all sides.
4. Wrap each 'sausage' in a cabbage leaf, tuck in the ends and secure with wooden cocktail sticks.
5. Preheat the oven to 200 °C (400 °F), lightly grease a large ovenproof dish and fill with the stuffed cabbage rolls. Pour over the leftover gravy, sprinkle with the dried breadcrumbs and bake for 20 minutes in the centre of the oven, adding a little stock or butter if the sauce dries out too much.
6. Serve with plain boiled rice or with creamy mashed potatoes.

Curly kale with smoked sausage

(Stamppot van boerenkool met worst)

1 kg (2 lb) (2 pounds) curly kale
1½ kg (3 lb) (3 pounds) potatoes
salt
400-500 g (12-16 oz) (12-16 ounces) smoked boiling sausage
30 g (1 oz) (2 tbs) butter
3-6 tbs (2-5 tbs) (2-5 tbs) milk or thin cream

1. Wash the kale, strip the leaves away from the stalks and chop them as finely as possible. Put them into the pan with a little water and salt to taste, bring to the boil, cover the pan and simmer for about 8 minutes or until they are half cooked. Drain well.
2. Peel the potatoes and cut into rough pieces. Put them into a large pan, cover them with the drained kale and season with a little salt. Pour in sufficient water to half cover the vegetables and place the sausage on top of the kale.
3. Cover the pan, bring slowly to the boil, reduce the heat and simmer gently for 30-35 minutes or until the potatoes are soft.
4. Remove the sausage from the pan, drain off the cooking liquid and reserve for later. Mash the kale with the potatoes and add the milk or cream and sufficient of the cooking liquid to make a smooth puree. Pile the mixture into a warm serving dish.
5. Slice the sausage and arrange the slices on top of the mashed vegetables. Serve immediately with gravy leftover from roast meat.

Variation:
Use 400 g (12 oz) (12 ounces) lightly salted streaky bacon instead of the boiling sausage. Cut into small cubes and fry gently to render out the fat. Spoon the crispy cubes of bacon, together with the melted fat into the mashed vegetables just before serving.

Note:
Smoked boiling sausage is very popular in Holland, Germany and Eastern Europe. Use any type which is available in your area.

Many butchers make their own fresh and smoked sausage.

Sauerkraut with bacon and potatoes

(Stamppot van zuurkool met spek)

1½ kg (3 lb) (3 pounds) potatoes
salt
600-700 g (1¼ – 1½ lb) (1¼ – 1½ pounds) sauerkraut, matured in wine
approx. 400 g (14 oz) (14 ounces) piece of lightly smoked, streaky bacon
30 g (1 oz) (2 tbs) butter
3-6 tbs (2-5 tbs) (2-5 tbs) milk or thin cream

1. Peel the potatoes and cut into rough pieces. Put them into a large pan with sufficient water to just cover them.
2. Pile the sauerkraut on top of the potatoes and separate the strands with a fork.
3. Place the bacon on top of the sauerkraut, cover the pan and bring slowly to the boil. Reduce the heat and simmer gently for about 30 minutes.
4. Remove the bacon from the pan and slice it thickly. Drain off the cooking liquid and reserve for later. Mash the potatoes with the sauerkraut and add the butter, milk or cream and sufficient of the cooking liquid to make a smooth mixture. Turn into a warm dish and cover with sliced bacon.

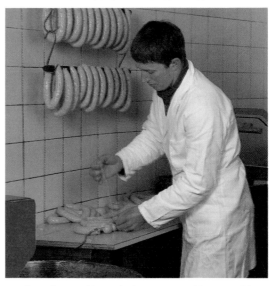

Sauerkraut with mashed potatoes and bacon – this can also be served with smoked sausage.

Cabbage and potato mash

(Stamppot van groene kool)

1½ kg (3 lb) (3 pounds) potatoes
approx. 1½ kg (3 lb) (3 pounds) green or white
cabbage
salt
1 tsp (½ tsp) (½ tsp) ground caraway seeds
2½ dl (8 fl oz) (1 cup) milk
40 g (1½ oz) (3 tbs) melted butter
1 tsp (½ tsp) (½ tsp) freshly ground pepper
1 tsp (½ tsp) (½ tsp) grated nutmeg

1. Peel and wash the potatoes, cut them into small pieces and put them into a large pan with a little water.
2. Remove the thick stalk and the outside leaves of the cabbage, quarter and cut into thin strips.
3. Season the potatoes with salt to taste and ground caraway and pile the shredded cabbage on top. Cover the pan, bring the contents slowly to the boil and then simmer gently for about 30 minutes, adding a little extra water if necessary.
4. Drain and reserve the liquid. Mash the cabbage and potatoes until smooth.
5. Mix the milk with the drained cooking liquid and melted butter and beat into the mashed vegetables.
6. Season with plenty of freshly ground pepper and (freshly) grated nutmeg. Serve immediately with pan-fried schnitzels or lamb or pork chops.

Variation:
Any type of cabbage can be used in this recipe.

Note:
Caraway can be purchased as whole seeds or ready ground. It is one of the best known and one of the oldest spices found all over Europe and tastes particularly good with cabbage and also with potatoes. It can easily be grown in the garden or on a sunny windowsill. It is not essential to this recipe and can be omitted if wished.

Dutch shepherd's pie

(Filosoof)

for the creamed potatoes:
approx. 1 kg (2 lb) (2 pounds) cold boiled potatoes
approx. 2½ dl (8 fl oz) (1 cup) milk
40 g (1½ oz) (3 tbs) melted butter
grated nutmeg
1 tsp (½ tsp) (½ tsp) freshly ground black pepper
dried breadcrumbs
1 tbs (½ tbs) (½ tbs) butter

for the meat sauce:
3 medium onions
50 g (2 oz) (4 tbs) butter
approx. 300 g (12 oz) (12 ounces) cold meat
1 bay leaf
2 cloves
pinch ground allspice
2-3 dl (7-10 fl oz) (⅞-1¼ cups) gravy or meat stock

1. Cream the potatoes with the milk, melted butter, nutmeg and pepper and set aside whilst you prepare the meat sauce.
2. Peel and finely chop the onions. Heat half of the butter and sauté the onions until soft. Meanwhile, chop the meat into small pieces and stir it into the sautéed onion.
3. Add the bay leaf, cloves, allspice and gravy or stock, cover the pan and simmer gently for approximately 50 minutes.
4. Preheat the oven to 200 °C (400 °F) when the meat sauce is almost cooked.
5. Remove the bay leaf and the cloves. Fill a lightly greased ovenproof dish with layers of creamed potato and meat sauce, starting and finishing with a layer of potato.
6. Sprinkle with dried breadcrumbs and dot with flakes of butter.
7. Bake for 15 minutes or until the surface is golden brown and crisp and serve with a fresh seasonal salad and apple or apricot sauce.

Variation:
Add 3-4 peeled, cored and sliced cooking apples to this Dutch style shepherd's pie. The resulting dish is known as Hunter's pie (Jachtschotel) in Holland.

Add the sliced apples when layering up the creamed potato and meat sauce, starting and ending with a layer of potato. Complete the dish as described above.

Thinly sliced boiled potatoes can be used instead of the creamed potato. Boil the potatoes in their skins and then peel and slice cold.

Another variation would be to use frozen røsti instead of creamed potatoes. There is no need to thaw before cooking – simply increase the baking time from 15 to 30 minutes.

Leftover cooked vegetables (cauliflower, broccoli, leeks, tomatoes, sprouts etc.) can also be added to make a more substantial dish.

Use grated cheese instead of dried breadcrumbs as a topping and flash the cooked shepherd's pie under a hot grill to brown the cheese.

Savoury beanpot

(Vijfschaft)

250 g (8 oz) (1½ cups) brown or kidney beans
500 g (1 lb) (1 pound) large carrots
3 medium onions
1 kg (2 lb) (2 pounds) potatoes
2 medium cooking apples
1 tsp (½ tsp) (½ tsp) savory
salt
freshly ground pepper
2 tbs (1½ tbs)(1½ tbs) cornflower or cornstarch

1. Wash the beans, cover with cold water and soak overnight. Cook the beans for 1½ hours in the water in which they were soaked, drain but leave just enough of the liquid in the pan to cover the cooked beans.
2. Peel and thinly slice or dice the carrots.
3. Peel and finely chop or thinly slice the onions.
4. Peel the potatoes and cut into large chunks.
5. Peel and core the apples and cut into small pieces.
6. Add the carrots and onions to the cooked beans, cover the pan and simmer for about 15 minutes.
7. Add the potatoes and apples, season with savory, salt and pepper, cover the pan and simmer for a further 15 minutes.
8. Drain the cooking liquid, but reserve 3 dl (½ pt) (1¼ cups) for the sauce. Thicken the sauce with the cornflour and add a dash of cream or milk if wished.

Variation:
Add a dash of cream or milk to the beanpot instead of making a sauce. Small pieces of crispy fried bacon can also be added for extra flavour.

Note:
Nobody in Holland is quite sure how this dish got it's name 'Vijfschaft'. It probably refers to the fact that the dish contains five main ingredients, but one well known Dutch dictionary describes 'vijfschaft' as a sturdy piece of cloth, embroidered with linen and woollen threads and bound with satin which was woven on a loom requiring five shuttles. This was worn by farmers and their wives.

Sweet and sour brown beans with bacon and apple

(Bruine bonen met appel, stroop en spek)

500 g (1 lb) (3 cups) brown or kidney beans
250 g (8 oz) (8 ounces) dried apples
salt
2 dl (7 fl oz) (⅞ cup) treacle or molasses
1 dl (3⅓ fl oz) (½ cup) cider vinegar
1 tbs (½ tbs)(½ tbs) butter
200 g (8 oz) (8 ounces) lean streaky bacon

1. Rinse the beans and the dried apples and soak overnight in plenty of cold water.
2. The next day, season with a little salt to taste and bring to the boil in the water in which they were soaked. Cover the pan and simmer gently for about 1½ hours, or until the beans are tender.
3. Mix the treacle with the vinegar in a small heavy based pan and heat gently, stirring all the time.
4. Drain the cooked beans and apples and pile into a warm serving dish. Spoon the treacle sauce through the beans, taking care that the beans and slices of apple remain whole.
5. Cover the dish and keep warm. Cut the bacon into thin strips and fry until crisp and golden brown in the hot butter.
6. Stir the bacon into the beans and serve hot.

Green beans with bacon

(Sperzieboontjes met spek)

500 g (1 lb) (1 pound) lean streaky bacon, thickly sliced
25 g (1 oz) (2 tbs) butter
approx. 750 g (12 oz) (12 ounces) green beans
1 dl (3½ fl oz) (½ cup) (vegetable)stock (see p. 17)
salt
grated nutmeg
pinch ground savory
freshly ground black pepper
3 firm pears
pinch ground cinnamon
1 dl (3½ fl oz) (½ cup) cream or milk

1. Cut the bacon into thin strips and fry golden brown and crisp in the hot butter in a heavy based frying pan. Reduce the heat.
2. Wash and drain the beans and break into short pieces, about 4 cm (1½ inches) long. Add them to the bacon, together with 1 dl (3½ fl oz) (½ cup) water and the stock.
3. Season with salt, nutmeg, savory and pepper.
4. Peel and core the pears and cut into large chunks. Add to the pan, cover and simmer gently for about 40 minutes or until the beans and pear are tender.
5. Season with a pinch of cinnamon and stir in the cream.
6. Serve with floury boiled potatoes or creamy mashed potatoes.

Note:
This recipe comes from the north of Holland and is known locally as 'Beantsjes mei spek'. It is a simple dish, prepared from home grown fruit and vegetables and is often made in the early autumn when the pears are still firm.

Tip:
Apples or leftover stewed pears can also be used instead of fresh ones. Add leftover stewed pears (see p. 69) towards the end of the cooking time.

Naked bottoms in the grass, a tempting dish of beans.

Naked bottoms in the green grass

(Blote billetjes in het groene gras)

A charming name for a delicious combination of haricot and sliced runner beans

300 g (12 oz) (2 cups) haricot beans
salt
1-2 bay leaves
½ tsp (¼ tsp) (¼ tsp) peppercorns
500 g (1 lb)(1 pound) runner beans
1 kg (2 lb) (2 pounds) potatoes
1 smoked boiling sausage
30 g (1 oz) (2 tbs) butter
1 dl (3½ fl oz) (½ cup) thin cream
freshly ground pepper
grated nutmeg
1 tsp (½ tsp) (½ tsp) savory

1. Rinse the haricot beans and soak overnight in plenty of cold water. Cook them the next day for 1 hour in the water in which they were soaked, season with salt, bay leaves and lightly crushed peppercorns.
2. String the runner beans and slice fairly thinly.
3. Peel the potatoes and cut into chunks.
4. Put the potatoes into a large heavy based pan, add a little water and pile the runner beans on top.
5. Place the sausage on top of the beans, cover the pan and bring the contents to the boil. Simmer gently for about 30 minutes until the vegetables are cooked.
6. Remove the sausage from the pan and keep it warm. Drain the vegetables and mash the potatoes with the beans.
7. Stir in the butter and the cream and then spoon the cooked and drained haricot beans through the mashed vegetables.
8. Season with pepper, nutmeg and savory and serve with the warm, sliced sausage.

Hotchpotch

(Hutspot met klapstuk)

See photo on page 84-85.

500 g (1 lb) (1 pound) lean beef (flank)
salt
1¼ kg (2½ lb) (2½ pounds) large carrots
1½ kg (3 lb) (3 pounds) potatoes
400-500 g (¾ – 1 lb) (¾ – 1 pound) onions
1 tsp (½ tsp) (½ tsp) freshly ground black pepper
25 g (1 oz) (2 tbs) butter
1 dl (3½ fl oz) (½ cup) thin cream

1. Put the beef in a large pan with approximately 4 dl (14 fl oz) (1¾ cups) water. Add a little salt to taste, cover the pan, bring to the boil and then reduce the heat and simmer gently for about 1½ hours, or until the meat is tender.
2. Peel and slice the carrots.
3. Peel the potatoes and cut into chunks.
4. Peel and roughly chop the onions. Add the prepared vegetables to the pan 30 minutes before the beef is cooked.
5. Remove the pan from the heat, lift out the meat and set aside on a warm plate. Drain off the cooking liquid and reserve for later. Mash the vegetables to a smooth puree.
6. Season well with freshly ground black pepper and salt and stir in the butter, cream and a little of the cooking liquid to make a fairly moist mixture.
7. Slice the meat or cut it into small chunks and serve with the piping hot mashed vegetables.

Tip:
Smoked boiling sausage can be used instead of flank – pile the chopped vegetables into a large pan with enough water to half cover them. Place the sausage on top and cook for 30 minutes or until the vegetables are soft. Complete the recipe as described above.

Haricot beans with bacon and carrots

(Leidse hutspot)

approx. 500 g (1 lb) (3 cups) haricot beans
400-500 g (14-16 oz) (14-16 ounce) piece of lean streaky bacon
1½ kg (3 lb) (3 pounds) large carrots
1 kg (2 lb) (2 pounds) onions
salt, freshly ground pepper

1. Soak the beans overnight in plenty of cold water.
2. Cut the bacon into cubes. Put the beans, the water in which they were soaked and the cubed bacon into a large pan, bring to the boil, cover and simmer for about 40 minutes.
3. Peel the carrots and slice thinly or cut into small cubes.
4. Peel and thinly slice the onions.
5. Add the carrots and onions to the beans and simmer gently for a further 30 minutes.
6. Drain off any excess cooking liquid and mix the ingredients thoroughly. Season with a little salt and pepper if necessary and serve hot.

Note:
'Hutspot' is still traditionally eaten on the 3rd of October in the city of Leiden in west Holland. Most families prefer the first of these two recipes, but a few still prepare the original 16th century version. The story behind the famous 'Leidse Hutspot': The city of Leiden had been under Spanish siege for several months when the Spanish soldiers suddenly left their camps outside the city walls. A small orphan, Cornelis Joppenz, was sent to spy out the land and in one of the deserted camps he found a pan full of stewed meat, beans, carrots and onions. This dish was unknown to the inhabitants of Leiden, but after all those months of near starvation, they were grateful to the boy for finding it. The inhabitants of Leiden still celebrate the end of the Spanish siege on October 3rd by serving 'Hutspot'. Originally it was made with beans, parsnips, carrots and other root vegetables, but with the introduction of the potato in Holland in the 18th century, the recipe gradually changed to the one served today.

Sweet and sour peas with apples and raisins

(Kapucijners met appel en rozijnen)

500 g (1 lb) (3 cups) dried marrowfat peas
250 g (8 oz) (8 ounces) dried apples
150 g (6 oz) (1 cup) sultanas or raisins
salt
2 tbs (1 tbs) (1 tbs) honey
1 tbs (½ tbs)(½ tbs) cider vinegar
1 tsp (½ tsp) (½ tsp) vanilla sugar

1. Rinse the peas and apples and soak them overnight in plenty of cold water.
2. The next day, bring them to the boil in the water in which they were soaked, add the sultanas and salt to taste, cover and simmer for about 1½ hours or until the peas are tender.
3. Mix the honey, cider vinegar and vanilla sugar in a heavy based pan and heat gently for 1-2 minutes.
4. Spoon the peas, apples and sultanas carefully through the honey sauce and serve immediately with creamed potatoes and fried pork chops.

Apple and potato mash

(Hete bliksem)

1½ kg (3 lb) (3 pounds) potatoes
1 kg (2 lb) (2 pounds) tart apples
40 g (1½ oz) (3 tbs) butter
2 tbs (1 tbs)(1 tbs) milk
salt
freshly ground black pepper

1. Peel the potatoes and cut them into quarters. Cut large potatoes into 6 pieces.
2. Peel and core the apples and cut them into large chunks.
3. Put the potatoes into a large pan with sufficient water to half cover them and pile the chunks of apple on top. Add the butter and bring the contents of the pan slowly to the boil.
4. Cover and simmer gently for about 30 minutes, or until the potatoes are cooked, adding a little extra water if necessary. Drain and reserve the cooking liquid.
5. Mash the potatoes with the apples and a dash of milk – moisten the mixture with a little of the cooking liquid if necessary. Season with salt and pepper.
6. Pile the potato mixture into a warm dish and serve with fried sausages or thickly sliced fried black pudding.

Smoked sausage with prunes and barley

(Pagaste)

An unusual recipe from the east of Holland

250 g (8 oz) (8 ounces) prunes
250 g (8 oz) (1 ⅔ cups) pearl barley
125 g (4 oz) (¾ cup) raisins or currants
1 large smoked boiling sausage
2-3 tbs (1-2 tbs) (1-2 tbs) treacle, syrup or molasses
1 tsp (½ tsp) (½ tsp) vanilla sugar

1. Cover the prunes with cold water and soak them overnight. Drain and reserve the water in which they were soaked.
2. Put the barley and the water from the prunes in a heavy based pan and simmer gently until the barley is cooked. Use quick cooking barley if available – this will only require cooking for about 20 minutes.
3. Add the prunes, raisins and sausage 15 minutes before the barley is cooked.
4. Drain off any excess liquid, remove the sausage from the pan and cut into fairly thick slices. Stir the treacle into the cooked barley mixture and add vanilla sugar to taste. Serve with the sliced sausage and a glass of chilled lager.

Variation:
If smoked boiling sausage is not available, use 500 g (1 lb) (1 pound) of frankfurters or knakwurst instead.

Hotchpotch – a delicious traditional Dutch meal
(see p. 84-85).

Vanilla custard

(Vanillevla)

1 l (1¾ pts) (4 cups) milk
½ vanilla pod
2 eggs
60 g (2 oz) (¼ cup) sugar
20 g (¾ oz) (2 tbs) cornflour or cornstarch

1. Bring the milk to the boil with the vanilla pod in a heavy based pan, remove from the heat and leave to infuse for 30 minutes.
2. Beat the eggs with the sugar until they are foamy and blend in the cornflour. Stir a few spoonfuls of the vanilla milk into the egg mixture and then return this to the milk in the pan, stirring all the time.
3. Heat the custard gently for about 5 minutes, stirring continuously, but do not allow it to boil. Use a double boiler if preferred.
4. Remove the vanilla pod and leave the custard to cool, stirring occasionally to prevent a skin from forming on the surface. Serve cold either on it's own or with chopped fresh or canned fruit. See recipe for Custard on p. 88.

Variation:
The above recipe can also be adapted to make a chocolate custard. Beat the eggs with 100 g (4 oz) (½ cup) sugar and blend in 50 g (2 oz) (⅓ cup) cocoa powder and the cornflour. Complete as above. For a harlequin custard, combine vanilla and chocolate custard in an attractive glass dish or in a tall glass for a harlequin effect. Garnish with a little whipped cream. Plain yoghurt and vanilla custard can be combined in a similar fashion – the Dutch call this a 'vlaflip'.

Note:
A wide range of ready made custards in various flavours and dairy desserts are available in all dairies and supermarkets in Holland. They are very popular as quick desserts.

Caramel coffee custard

(Hopjesvla)

Another firm favourite in Holland

250 g (8 oz) (1 cup) sugar
50 g (2 oz) (⅓ cup) cornflour or cornstarch
2 egg yolks
8 dl (1⅓ pts) (3½ cups) milk
5 dl (17 fl oz) (2 cups) thin cream
2 dl (7 fl oz) (⅞ cup) strong sweet coffee

1. Melt the sugar in a heavy based pan and heat gently until it starts to caramelize. Remove the pan from the heat and allow to cool slightly. Stir in 2 spoonfuls of cold water.
2. Blend the cornflour with the lightly beaten egg yolks and 3 spoonfuls of cold milk in a small basin.
3. Add the rest of the milk to the caramel and bring slowly to the boil. Stir a little of the hot caramel milk into the cornflour and egg blend.
4. Pour this back into the hot caramel milk in the pan, stirring all the time and cook gently, still stirring for about 3 minutes or until the custard thickens. Use a double boiler if preferred.
5. Stir in the thin cream and the coffee, remove the pan from the heat.
6. Leave the custard to cool, stirring occasionally to prevent a skin from forming and serve cold.

Four custard desserts – combine two flavours for an attractive result.

Custard

(Custardvla)

1 l (1¾ pts) (4 cups) milk
approx. 50 g (2 oz) (½ cup) custard powder
50 g (2 oz) (¼ cup) sugar

1. Bring the milk to the boil in a heavy based pan.
2. Blend the custard powder with a few spoonfuls of warm milk and stir this into the hot milk in the pan. Add the sugar.
3. Cook the custard gently for about 3 minutes, stirring from time to time, remove the pan from the heat and allow the custard to cool. Stir it occasionally to prevent a skin from forming.

Tip:
Delicious with chopped fresh fruit, stewed rhubarb or stewed apple, chocolate or caramel coffee custard, sponge fingers or ice cream wafers.

Variation:
Pour a little custard pudding over a scoop of vanilla ice cream and decorate with a whirl of fresh whipped cream.

Caramel custard

(Caramelvla)

8 dl (1⅓ pts) (3½ cups) milk
½ vanilla pod
175 g (6 oz) (¾ cup) sugar
2 eggs
35 g (1¼ oz) (3½ tbs) cornflour or cornstarch

1. Bring the milk and the vanilla pod to the boil in a heavy based pan, remove the pan from the heat and leave to infuse for 30 minutes.
2. Melt the sugar in a separate heavy based pan and heat until it starts to caramelize.
3. Remove the pan from the heat and allow the caramel to cool slightly. Stir in 2 spoonfuls of water.
4. Remove the vanilla pod from the milk and pour this over the caramel. Stir and heat gently until the caramel has dissolved.
5. Separate the eggs and beat the yolks with the cornflour. Add 3 spoonfuls of the caramel milk.
6. Stir this into the caramel milk in the pan and heat gently, stirring continuously for about 4 minutes until the custard thickens. Use a double boiler if preferred.
7. Remove the pan from the heat and allow the custard to cool, stirring occasionally to prevent a skin from forming on the surface.

Semolina mould with fruit sauce – a favourite dessert in Holland.

Semolina mould

(Griesmeelpudding)

8 dl (1¹/₃ pts) (3¹/₂ cups) milk
¹/₂ vanilla pod
80 g (3 oz) (¹/₂ cup) semolina
70 g (2¹/₂ oz) (¹/₃ cup) sugar
2 medium eggs

1. Bring the milk to the boil with the vanilla pod in a heavy based pan.
2. Sprinkle the semolina and the sugar into the milk and stir well. Cook gently until the semolina has thickened and the grains are soft. Remove the vanilla pod.
3. Cool the semolina, separate the eggs and beat the yolks into the cooled semolina.
4. Beat the egg whites until they are stiff and dry, fold them through the semolina mixture and turn into a well rinsed jelly mould. Leave until completely cold.
5. Turn the mould out onto a suitable plate and garnish with blackberries and/or red currants.

Tip:
Semolina mould can also be served with a fruit sauce, see the Sauce chapter on p. 26 for suitable recipes or serve with a commercial bottled fruit sauce.

Ratafia pudding with raisins

(Bitterkoekjespudding met rozijnen)

See photo on p. 92-93.

6 dl (1 pt) (2½ cups) milk
4 slices stale white bread, crusts removed
125 g (5 oz) (5 ounces) ratafia biscuits
3 eggs
75 g (3 oz) (⅓ cup) sugar
100 g (4 oz) (⅔ cup) raisins
1 tbs (½ tbs)(½ tbs) soft butter
dried breadcrumbs

1. Heat the milk gently in a large heavy based pan.
2. Cut the bread into small cubes and soak the bread and ratafia biscuits in the hot milk. Mash well to make a smooth mixture.
3. Separate the eggs and beat the yolks with the sugar. Beat the egg whites until stiff and dry.
4. Stir the washed and dried raisins into the beaten egg yolks, spoon this through the ratafia mixture and fold in the beaten egg whites.
5. Lightly grease a pudding basin (with lid) with the softened butter and dust the inside with dried breadcrumbs. Shake out any excess breadcrumbs.
6. Pile the ratafia mixture into the basin, cover with the lid, or with aluminium foil and place in a large pan with sufficient boiling water to come up to the rim of the basin.
7. Adjust the heat so that the water is just simmering and steam the pudding for 1½ hours. Remove the lid, set aside for 5 minutes and then loosen the edges of the pudding with a palette knife.
8. Turn the pudding out onto a warm plate and garnish it with a few extra ratafia biscuits.
9. Serve warm or cold with or without a fruit sauce.

Tip:
Strawberry, blueberry or a sauce made from mixed summer fruits would be a suitable accompaniment.

The Hague bluff

(Haagse bluf)

2 dl (7 fl oz) (⅞ cup) blackcurrant juice
80 g (3 oz) (⅓ cup) sugar
2 egg whites
4 sponge fingers or ice cream wafers

1. Put the juice, sugar and egg whites into a large basin and beat with an electric handmixer until the mixture resembles whipped cream.
2. Spoon it into glass dishes and serve with sponge fingers or ice cream wafers.

Note:
It is said that the inhabitants of the Hague (known as Hagenaars) are often inclined to put on airs and graces. Rumour has it that they will go shopping with an empty violin case instead of with a shopping bag in order to appear cultured! Many people believe that this recipe was invented by a Hagenaar who wanted to bluff his guests into thinking that they were eating dishes of fruit flavoured whipped cream.

Barley pudding

(Watergruwel)

75 g (3 oz) (½ cup) pearl barley
75 g (3 oz) (½ cup) raisins
75 g (3 oz) (½ cup) currants
the peel of 1 lemon
½ stick cinnamon
approx. 3½ dl (12 fl oz) (1½ cups) blackcurrant juice
approx. 100 g (4 oz) (½ cup) sugar

1. Wash the barley and soak overnight in approximately 7 dl (1¼ pts) (3 cups) water.
2. The next day, bring the barley, raisins, currants, lemon peel and cinnamon to the boil in the same water.
3. Reduce the heat and simmer gently for about 1 hour.
4. Add the blackcurrant juice and sugar to taste and

simmer for a further 5 minutes.

5. Remove the lemon peel and the cinnamon and serve the barley pudding hot or cold – garnish with a little fresh or lightly soured cream if so wished.

Tip:

Quick cooking barley is also available – this will save a lot of preparation and cooking time; follow the instructions on the packet.

Variation:

Add a little chopped candied peel or pre-soaked dried apricots to the pudding for an extra fruity flavour. These should be cooked in the pudding for about 20 minutes.

Cherry pudding

(Kersenpap)

800 g (1½ lb) (1½ pounds) tart cherries
approx. 50 g (2 oz) (4 tbs) butter
2 tbs (1 tbs) (1 tbs) ground cinnamon
2 tbs (1 tbs) (1 tbs) cherry liqueur
75 g (3 oz) (⅔ cup) flour
1 l (1¾ pts) (4 cups) buttermilk
4 tbs (3 tbs) (3 tbs) caster sugar
2 liqueur glasses of Dutch brandy (brandewijn) or kirsch

1. Wash and stone the cherries and drain in a colander.
2. Melt the butter in a large heavy based pan and stew the cherries over a low heat.
3. Sprinkle in the cinnamon, add the cherry liqueur, cover the pan and shake over a low heat until the cherries are soft.
4. Meanwhile, blend the flour with 5 spoonfuls of the buttermilk and then gradually stir in the rest. Bring slowly to the boil in a separate pan, whisking all the time to make a smooth sauce.
5. Stir the stewed cherries into the buttermilk sauce and add sugar to taste.
6. Spoon the cherry pudding into 4 warm soup plates, pour over the brandy or kirsch and serve with sponge fingers or with rusks.

Rice pudding

(Rijstebrij)

125 g (5 oz) (¾ cup) pudding rice
1 l (1¾ pts) (4 cups) milk
salt
lemon peel
soft brown or vanilla sugar
ground cinnamon

1. Wash the rice in a sieve until the water runs clear.
2. Pour the milk into a heavy based pan and bring it slowly to the boil. Add a pinch of salt and a small piece of lemon peel.
3. Stir in the washed rice and simmer very gently for about 1 hour until the rice is cooked. Stir the pudding frequently to prevent it from sticking to the base of the pan.
4. Serve in a warm dish or in separate dishes and sprinkle with soft brown or vanilla sugar and ground cinnamon.

Lamb's pudding

(Lammetjespap)

Often served to children as a warm cereal dish

approx. 75 g (3 oz) (⅔ cup) flour
1 l (1¾ pts) (4 cups) milk
salt
1 small egg

1. Blend the flour with about 1 dl (3½ fl oz) (½ cup) cold milk.
2. Bring the rest of the milk to the boil and add the flour blend, stirring all the time. Simmer gently for 3-4 minutes, still stirring, until the mixture has thickened.
3. Add salt to taste and lightly beat the egg. Remove the pan from the heat, stir in the beaten egg and serve immediately.

On following pages: ratafia pudding with raisins – attractive with a delicious flavour.

Desserts

Rolled oat porridge

(Havermoutpap)

1 l (1¾ pts) (4 cups) milk
salt
approx. 80 g (3 oz) (¾ cup) rolled oats
sugar, treacle, molasses or maple syrup to taste

1. Bring the milk to the boil, add salt to taste and sprinkle in the rolled oats. Reduce the heat and simmer gently for 15-20 minutes, stirring all the time until the porridge has thickened.
2. Serve with sugar or syrup to taste.

Tip:
The quick cooking variety of rolled oats can also be used; follow the instructions on the packet.

Curd cheese

(Hangop)

A low-fat fresh dessert cheese

3 l (5¼ pts) (16 cups) buttermilk
4-6 rusks or graham crackers
caster or soft brown sugar
ground cinnamon

1. Line a colander with a large piece of clean, wet butter muslin.
2. Place the colander over a large bowl or pan and fill it with the buttermilk. The whey, or watery part of the buttermilk, will drain through the muslin, leaving behind a thick curd.
3. Scrape the curd away from the sides of the colander, making it easier for the whey to drain through.
4. Spread the curd thickly onto rusks or graham crackers and sprinkle with sugar and ground cinnamon to taste.

Tip:
The curd can be enriched by adding a few spoonfuls of whipped cream or lightly soured cream. Serve with honey or jam.

Barley pudding with buttermilk

(Karnemelkse gortepap)

125 g (5 oz) (¾ cup) barley
1 l (1¾ pts) (4 cups) buttermilk
salt
sugar, treacle or molasses

1. Wash the barley and soak overnight in plenty of water.
2. Drain and bring slowly to the boil with the buttermilk and a little salt to taste.
3. Simmer the barley for about 1½ hours until the grains are tender, stir frequently to prevent it from sticking to the base of the pan.
4. Serve with sugar or syrup to taste.

Tip:
Quick cooking barley can be used to reduce the cooking time. Follow the instructions on the packet.

Frisian buttermilk porridge

(Friese karnemelkse pap)

approx. 70 g (3 oz)(⅔ cup) flour
1 l (1¾ pts) (4 cups) buttermilk
150-200 g (6-8 oz) (6-8 ounces) thinly sliced streaky bacon
treacle, molasses or corn syrup to taste

1. Blend the flour with a little of the cold buttermilk and then gradually stir in the rest, making sure that there are no lumps in the mixture.
2. Bring the blended flour and buttermilk to the boil, stirring all the time, reduce the heat and simmer gently for about 5 minutes.
3. Render the fat out of the bacon over a low heat.
4. Spoon the porridge into warm dishes and pile the bacon onto a warm plate. Serve with treacle, molasses or corn syrup to taste.

Farmhouse waffles

(Boerenwafels)

4 eggs
5-6 tbs (4-5 tbs) (4-5 tbs) milk
6 rusks or graham crackers
butter for frying
soft brown sugar
ground cinnamon

1. Lightly beat the eggs with the milk in a wide, shallow dish and soak the rusks in this mixture.
2. Heat a little butter or margarine in a large frying pan and fry the soaked rusks, three at a time, until golden brown on both sides. Fry the remaining rusks in the same way.
3. Serve the waffles on warm plates and sprinkle immediately with sugar and ground cinnamon to taste.

Tip:
Spread the waffles with a little jam or fruit jelly instead of sprinkling them with sugar and cinnamon; or pipe a rosette of whipped cream in the centre of each one and garnish with a glacé cherry.

Note:
This dessert comes from the eastern Dutch province of Drenthe and used to be served as a snack to the hard working farm labourers. Instead of rusks, you can use stale white bread with the crusts removed.

Egg pancakes

(Eierpannekoeken)

250 g (8 oz) (2 cups) self raising flour
½ tsp (¼ tsp) (¼ tsp) salt
5 dl (17 fl oz) (2 cups) milk
4 eggs
butter for frying
treacle, molasses, corn syrup or jam to taste

1. Sift the flour and salt into a large bowl. Make a hollow in the top of the flour and pour in a little of the milk.
2. Gradually beat the milk into the flour, working from the centre out to the sides of the bowl.
3. Beat in the eggs, one by one and gradually add the rest of the milk to make a smooth, pouring batter.
4. Melt a knob of butter in a heavy based or non-stick frying pan and pour in just enough batter to cover the base of the pan. Fry gently until the underside is golden brown, flip the pancake over and fry the other side.
5. Slide the pancake onto a warm plate and keep warm whilst the rest are being fried, or serve immediately with sugar, treacle, molasses, corn syrup, jam or stewed fruit.

Poffertjes

(Poffertjes; for more information see p. 109)

250 g (8 oz) (2 cups) self-raising flour
1-2 eggs
3½ dl (12 fl oz) (1½ cups) milk
pinch salt
1 tbs (½ tbs)(½ tbs) sugar
oil or butter for frying
icing sugar
extra butter for serving

1. Sift the flour into a large bowl and make a hollow in the top.
2. Break the eggs into the hollow, add a little of the milk and stir to make a smooth batter, working from the centre out to the sides of the bowl.
3. Gradually stir in the rest of the milk, add a little salt and sugar to taste and continue stirring and make a smooth pouring batter.
4. Lightly grease a 'poffertjes' pan with oil or melted butter and fill each indentation in the pan with a little of the batter. Do not allow it to flow over the edge.
5. Fry quickly and turn when the undersides are golden brown.
6. Pile onto small plates, dust liberally with icing sugar and serve with a knob of butter. 'Poffertjes' should be eaten as soon as they are cooked.

White bread

(Wittebrood)

1 kg (2 lb) (8 cups) white flour
20 g (1 tbs) (1 tbs) salt
40 g (1½ oz) (1½ ounces) fresh yeast or 20 g (¾ oz)
(2 tbs) dried yeast
2 tsp(1 tsp) (1 tsp) sugar
approx. 6 dl (1 pt) (2½ cups) warm milk
oil

1. Sift the flour and salt into a large bowl.
2. Cream the yeast and sugar with a little of the warm milk and leave until it starts to froth.
3. Make a hollow in the mound of flour and pour in the yeast mixture and the rest of the warm milk.
4. Gradually work the milk into the flour and knead to an elastic dough which easily comes away from the sides of the bowl.
5. Turn the dough onto a well floured work surface and knead for about 5 minutes.
6. Shape the dough into a ball, return it to the bowl, cover with a damp cloth and leave in a warm place for about 1 hour or until well risen. Knead the risen dough until smooth.
7. Lightly grease 1 large or two small loaf tins and shape the dough to fit the tin. Cover and leave to rise for 30 minutes. Preheat the oven to 230 °C (450 °F) 10 minutes before you wish to bake the bread.
8. Bake for about 35 minutes just below the centre of the oven until the bread is well risen and golden brown.
9. Brush the top of the loaf with water – this will give it a glaze. Remove it from the tin and allow to cool thoroughly before slicing.

Wholewheat bread

(Volkorenbrood)

See photo on p. 97

750 g (1½ lb) (6 cups) wholewheat flour
250 g (8 oz) (2 cups) white flour
approx. 6 dl (1 pt) (2½ cups) warm water or milk

50 g (2 oz) (2 ounces) fresh yeast or 25 g (1 oz)
(7 tsp) dried yeast
20 g (1 tbs) (1 tbs) salt
1 tsp (½ tsp) (½ tsp) sugar
oil

1. Sift the wholewheat flour, white flour and salt into a large bowl.
2. Cream the yeast and sugar with a little of the warm water or milk and leave until frothy.
3. Follow the recipe for white bread, starting at point 3.

Note:
Water will give a lighter result than milk when using wholewheat flour.

Poor knights

(Wentelteefjes)

8 slices stale bread
2 eggs
pinch salt
2 tbs (1 tbs) (1 tbs) sugar
ground cinnamon
3 dl (½ pt) (1¼ cups) milk
butter for frying
icing sugar

1. Remove the crusts from the bread. Beat the eggs with a pinch of salt, sugar and ground cinnamon to taste. Gradually stir in the milk.
2. Soak the bread for a few minutes in the egg mixture and heat a little butter in a large frying pan.
3. Fry the bread golden brown on both sides over a medium heat and serve immediately with a liberal sprinkling of icing sugar.

Tip:
Poor knights also taste good when served with jam.

Baking bread is a rewarding pastime. Here you see wholewheat loaves just before baking.

Crown loaf

(Driekoningenbrood)

500 g (1 lb) (4 cups) white flour
5 g (1 tsp) (1 tsp) salt
50 g (2 oz) (2 ounces) fresh yeast or 25 g (1 oz)
(7 tsp) dried yeast
15 g (½ oz) (4 tsp) vanilla sugar
2-2½ dl (7-8 fl oz) (7/8-1 cup) milk
100 g (4 oz) (½ cup) butter
2 egg yolks
approx. 125 g (5 oz) (¾ cup) sultanas
1 dl (3½ fl oz) (½ cup) liqueur (any sort)
100 g (4 oz) (1 cup) ground almonds
approx. 75 g (3 oz) (⅓ cup) sugar
grated peel of 1 lemon
juice of ½ lemon
1 whole almond
2 egg yolks
melted butter or milk for the glaze

1. Sift the flour and salt into a large bowl and make a hollow in the top.
2. Cream the yeast and vanilla sugar with half of the warm milk.
3. Melt the butter, stir in the egg yolks and mix with the creamed yeast.
4. Pour this mixture into the hollow in the flour, add the rest of the warm milk and gradually work the liquid ingredients into the flour to make a soft, elastic dough which easily comes away from the sides of the bowl.
5. Turn onto a well floured work surface and knead for about 5 minutes with cool hands. Shape the dough into a ball, return it to the basin, cover with a damp cloth and leave in a warm place for about 45 minutes or until well risen.
6. Soak the sultanas for 30 minutes in the liqueur. Grand Marnier or Cointreau would be a good choice.
7. Mix the ground almonds with the sugar, grated lemon peel and lemon juice and knead into the risen dough, together with the soaked sultanas and single almond.
8. Shape the dough into a ball, place on a greased baking sheet, cover with a damp cloth and leave to rise for about 30 minutes. Preheat the oven to

220 °C (425 °F) 10 minutes before you wish to bake the bread.
9. Using a knife or a sharp pair of kitchen scissors, cut around the edge of the ball of dough to form a crown and cut a star shape in the centre.
10. Bake the crown for about 45 minutes just below the centre of the oven until it is well risen and golden brown.
11. Brush the top liberally with the egg yolk, mixed with a little melted butter or milk and cool on a wire tray before slicing.

Bread pudding

(Broodpudding)

400 g (14 oz) (14 ounces) stale bread, crusts removed
approx. 8 dl (1⅓ pts) (3½ cups) milk
60 g (2 oz) (4 tbs) butter
125 g (5 oz) (½ cup) sugar
4-5 medium eggs
100 g (4 oz) (2/3 cup) raisins
75 g (3 oz) (½ cup) currants
1 tbs (½ tbs) (½ tbs) chopped candied peel
100 g (4 oz) (1 cup) grated apple
oil, dried breadcrumbs

1. Cut the bread into small cubes or crumble it in the food processor. Bring the milk to the boil in a heavy based pan and stir in the bread. Simmer gently for 4-5 minutes until it resembles thick porridge.
2. Cut the butter into small pieces and add them, together with the sugar, beaten eggs, raisins, currants, candied peel and apple.
3. Remove the pan from the heat before the mixture comes back to the boil. Lightly grease a large round cake tin or 2 small loaf tins with a little oil and dust the inside with dried breadcrumbs. Pile the mixture into the tin, cover with aluminium foil and steam for about 1½ hours.
4. Remove the pudding from the steamer, cool for about 5 minutes in the tin and then loosen the edges with a knife.
5. Turn the pudding out onto a warm dish and serve with a hot fruit, vanilla or chocolate sauce.

Easter bread

(Paasbrood)

See photo on p. 100-101.

200 g (7 oz) (1¼ cups) raisins
200 g (7 oz) (1¼ cups) currants
75 g (3 oz) (½ cup) candied peel
500 g (1 lb) (2 cups) flour
10 g (1 tsp) (1 tsp) salt
grated peel of 1 lemon
40 g (1½ oz) (1½ ounces) fresh yeast or 20 g (¾ oz)
(2 tbs) dried yeast
1½ dl (5 fl oz) (2/3 cup) warm milk
2 tsp (1 tsp) (1 tsp) sugar
1 egg
25 g (1 oz) (2 tbs) butter
butter and flour for preparing the loaf tin
approx. 250 g (8 oz) (8 ounces) ready made
marzipan

1. Cover the raisins and currants with a little hot water and soak for 30 minutes. Drain and pat dry with kitchen paper.
2. Mix the raisins, currants and candied peel in a small bowl.
3. Sift the flour with the salt into a large bowl and stir in the grated lemon peel.
4. Cream the yeast and sugar with the milk and leave in a warm place until frothy.
5. Make a hollow in the top of the flour and pour in the creamed yeast. Add the lightly beaten egg and melted butter.
6. Gradually work the liquid ingredients into the flour and knead to a soft, dough which easily comes away from the sides of the bowl.
7. Roll the dough out on a well floured work surface and then gather it up and knead it back into shape. Repeat this several times until the dough is elastic and easy to handle.
8. Shape into a ball, return it to the bowl, cover with a damp cloth and leave in a warm place for about 1 hour or until well risen.
9. Lightly grease a medium loaf tin with butter and dust the inside with a little flour.
10. Gradually knead the raisins and currants into the risen dough and shape into a rectangle, the

same size as the lenght of the tin.
11. Place a roll of marzipan along the centre of the rectangle, roll up the dough and place it in the tin with the seam on the underside. Cover with a damp cloth and leave in a warm place for about 45 minutes or until the dough has risen to the top of the tin.
12. Preheat the oven to 220 °C (425 °F) and bake the Easter bread just under the centre of the oven for about 45 minutes or until the loaf is well risen and golden brown.
13. Glaze the top of the loaf with a little water or melted butter, remove it from the tin and cool on a wire rack.
14. Dust the loaf liberally with icing sugar and slice fairly thickly.

Dutch bakers, like all other bakers, rise early to prepare the day's assortment of bread, rolls and cakes.

On the following pages: Easter bread is an integral part of the Easter celebration in Holland.

Loaves for palm sunday

(Palmpasenbrood)

600 g (1¼ lb) (5 cups) flour
12 g (2 tsp) (2 tsp) salt
25 g (1 oz) (1 ounce) fresh yeast or 12 g (½ oz)
(4 tsp) dried yeast, 1 tsp (½ tsp) (½ tsp) sugar
approx. 3½ dl (12 fl oz) (1½ cups) warm milk
1-2 eggs, milk for glazing

1. Prepare the bread dough as described in the recipe for white bread on page 96 and leave in a warm place to rise.
2. Weigh out approximately 600 g (1¼ lb) (1¼ pounds) risen dough and shape 500 g (1 lb) (1 pound) of this into 3 thin rolls. Plait these and join the ends to make a wheel. Divide the remaining 100 g (4 oz) (4 ounces) dough into four pieces and shape each into a long, thin roll. Use to make 'spokes' in the centre of the plaited wheel.
3. Shape approximately 200 g (7 oz) (7 ounces) risen dough into a large 'S' shape and flatten the base slightly to make a swan. Shape 3 smaller pieces of dough, approximately 40 g (1½ oz) (1½ ounces) in weight in the same way to make small swans.
4. Press a currant into the head of each swan to make the eyes, place all the shaped dough onto greased baking sheets, cover with damp cloths and leave in a warm place to rise for about 15 minutes.
5. Meanwhile, preheat the oven to 240 °C (460 °F). Bake the wheel and the swans for about 20 minutes

Loaves for Palm Sunday. In certain parts of Holland it is traditional to have a children's parade on Palm Sunday. All the children carry a decorated Palm cross.

just below the centre of the oven or until well risen and golden brown – the small swans may be ready a little sooner. Glaze with the beaten egg and milk and cool on a wire tray.
6. Cut two pieces of cane and tie them together to make a cross. Tie the wheel onto the centre of the cross. Tie the large swan onto the top piece of the cross and attach the small swans to the wheel with fine string or with wooden cocktail sticks.
7. Decorate the palm cross with leaves, coloured paper streamers or bows of ribbon and strings of dried prunes, dried apricots, currants and raisins.

Currant doughnuts

(Oliebollen)

makes approx. 25 doughnuts

Currant doughnuts are traditionally served up on New Year's Eve and are on sale all over Holland either at the local bakery or at colourful street stalls. The air is scented with the delicious sugary smell of frying doughnuts as everyone prepares for the New Year's Eve festivities. The evening is spent either with family or friends and as the clock strikes midnight fireworks are set off to celebrate the coming of the New Year.

400 g (14 oz) (3½ cups) flour
25 g (1 oz) (1 ounce) fresh yeast or 15 g (½ oz)
(4 tsp) dried yeast
3 dl (½ pt)(1¼ cups) warm milk
2 large eggs
1½ tbs (1 tbs) (1 tbs) sugar
20 g (¾ oz) (1½ tbs) melted butter
200 g (7 oz) (1¼ cup) currants and raisins mixed
50 g (2 oz) (⅓ cup) chopped mixed peel
1-2 tart apples
grated peel of 1 lemon
oil for deep frying
sifted icing sugar

1. Sift the flour into a large bowl and make a hollow in the top of the mound.
2. Cream the yeast with a little of the warm milk.
3. Beat the eggs with the sugar, add the creamed yeast and pour into the hollow in the flour. Leave for a few minutes in a warm place until the yeast mixture starts to froth. Add the rest of the warm milk and stir from the centre outwards, to make a smooth thick batter.
4. Melt the butter, mix the currants and raisins with the chopped peel and stir them with the butter into the batter.
5. Peel, core and finely chop the apples and add them to the batter, together with the finely grated lemon peel.
6. Mix well, cover the bowl with a damp cloth and leave for 30 minutes in a warm place until the batter is well risen.
7. Meanwhile heat the oil to a temperature of 180 °C (350 °F). Shape the risen batter with 2 greased dessert spoons into small balls and drop them into the hot fat. Fry no more than 5 doughnuts at a time, otherwise the fat will cool down too quickly.
8. Scoop the golden brown doughnuts out of the hot fat and drain well on kitchen paper. They should be soft on the inside with a crisp golden crust.
9. Dust liberally with sifted icing sugar and serve warm.

Apple fritters

(Appelbeignets)

Another Dutch speciality eaten on New Year's Eve.

makes approx. 20 fritters

150 g (6 oz) (1¼ cups) self raising flour
1 medium egg
approx. 2 dl (7 fl oz) (7/8 cup) milk
salt
approx. 8 cooking apples
oil or fat for deep frying
sifted icing sugar

1. Sift the flour into a mixing bowl and make a small hollow in the top.
2. Break the egg into the hollow and gradually stir in the egg and enough of the milk to make a smooth fritter batter. Add a pinch of salt to taste.
3. Peel and core the apples and cut into fairly thick slices, 1½ cm (½ inch).
4. Dip each slice into the batter and deep fry until golden brown in the hot fat or oil. Fry two or three at a time, depending on the size of the pan.
5. Remove them from the fat and drain well on kitchen paper.
6. Dust liberally with sifted icing sugar and serve warm.

Tip:
Apple fritters also taste delicious if they are spread with a thin layer of jam or jelly instead of with sugar.

Sugared almond slice

(Jan Hagel)

makes approx. 900 g (2 lb) (2 pounds) biscuits

400 g (14 oz) (3½ cups) self raising flour or plain
flour with 1½ tsp (1 tsp) (1 tsp) baking powder
approx. 150 g (6 oz) (1 cup) caster sugar
300 g (12 oz) (1½ cups) butter
1 lightly beaten egg
approx. 75 g (3 oz) (¾ cup) flaked almonds
40 g (1½ oz) (4 tbs) granulated or coffee sugar

1. Sift the flour and sugar into a bowl. Cut the butter into small pieces and rub it into the flour until it resembles fine breadcrumbs. Knead lightly to make a smooth dough. Roll the pastry out on a floured surface into a large rectangle approximately ½ cm (¼ inch) thick.
2. Preheat the oven to 170 °C (350 °F). Lift the pastry carefully onto a lightly greased baking sheet and brush the top with the beaten egg. Press the flaked almonds into the pastry and sprinkle with sugar.
3. Bake the almond slice for about 20 minutes in the centre of the oven or until it is light golden brown.
4. Leave the pastry to cool on the baking sheet for a few minutes and then cut it into rectangular or square pieces and cool on a wire tray. Store in an airtight tin.

Coconut macaroons

(Kokosmakarons)

makes approx. 400 g (14 oz) (14 ounces) macaroons

4 egg whites
pinch of salt
200 g (7 oz) (1⅓ cups) caster sugar
8 g (2 tsp) (2 tsp) vanilla sugar
approx. 100 g (4 oz) (1¼ cups) dessicated coconut
rice paper

1. Beat the egg whites with a pinch of salt until they are stiff and dry. Add the caster and vanilla sugar little by little and beat until the mixture is thick and glossy.
2. Stir in the coconut. Preheat the oven to approximately 150 °C (300 °F).
3. Line a baking sheet with pieces of rice paper and spoon small mounds of the coconut mixture onto the tray. Allow enough space in between the mounds for them to spread.
4. Bake for approximately 30 minutes in the centre of the oven or until the macaroons are light golden brown in colour.
5. Trim away the rice paper between the macaroons and cool them on a wire tray.

Butter crisps

(Arnhemse meisjes)

See photo on page 106-107.

makes approx. 500 g (1 lb) (1 pound) biscuits

200 g (7 oz) (1¾ cups) flour
200 g (7 oz) (7/8 cup) butter
salt
1 egg
80 g (3 oz) (½ cup) caster sugar.

1. Sift the flour and a pinch of salt into a large bowl. Cut the butter into small pieces.
2. Rub the butter into the flour until the mixture resembles fine breadcrumbs and then add sufficient ice cold water to make a firm dough. Add the water a little at a time, otherwise the dough may become too sticky.
3. Knead the dough lightly and roll it out on a floured surface to a rectangle about ½ cm (¼ inch) thick.
4. Fold the dough in three and roll it out again, this time a little thinner. Repeat this two more times and then wrap the pastry in plastic foil and leave in the refrigerator for about 30 minutes.
5. Fold, roll and 'rest' the dough three times in all.
6. Preheat the oven to 220 °C (425 °F) and then roll the pastry out to a thickness of 3 mm (⅛ inch). Stamp out small circles of dough with a round cutter or glass, 4 cm (1¾ inches) in diameter, roll them slightly to make an oval shape and lift them onto a damp baking sheet.
7. Lightly beat the egg with a spoonful of cold water and brush the tops of the biscuits with this mixture. Sprinkle them with a little sugar and bake for 20-25 minutes in the centre of the oven, or until crisp and golden brown.
8. Wait for 2 minutes before lifting the biscuits onto a wire tray and store in an airtight tin once they are completely cold.

Crispy heart waffles

(Vlinders)

See photo on page 106-107.

makes approx. 600 g (1¼ lb) (1¼ pounds) waffles

400 g (14 oz) (3½ cups) flour
pinch salt
approx. 100 g (4 oz) (½ cup) caster sugar
3 eggs
7 dl (1¼ pts) (3 cups) milk
oil or fat for frying
icing sugar

1. Sift the flour, salt and sugar into a large bowl. Break the eggs on top of the flour and gradually beat in the milk to make a smooth thick batter. This is best done with an electric handmixer.
2. Heat the oil or fat in a deep fryer and place a special heart shaped waffle iron in the fat for a few minutes. These small waffle irons are available from good hardware stores in Holland – any small waffle iron, suitable for using in a deep fryer can be used instead of the traditional heart or butterfly shaped one.
3. Dip the top side of the waffle iron into the batter and then plunge it into the hot oil or fat.
4. Fry the heart waffles until light golden brown, remove from the fat and shake the waffle out onto kitchen paper. Cool until crisp.
5. Sprinkle with sugar or serve with jam and syrup.

Variation:
Salted heart waffles can be made using 15 g (½ oz) (1 tbs) salt and 50 g (2 oz) (¼ cup) caster sugar instead of the amount of sugar given above.

On the following pages: A selection of Dutch cookies including butter crisps (left) and crispy heart waffles (centre).

Hazelnut cookies

(Friese hazelnootkoekjes)

makes approx. 650 g (1¼ lb) (1¼ pounds)

100 g (4 oz) (1 cup) blanched hazelnuts
150 g (6 oz) (¾ cup) soft butter
approx. 100 g (4 oz) (¾ cup) soft brown sugar
2 medium eggs
250 g (8 oz) (2 cups) flour
1 tsp (½ tsp) (½ tsp) ground cinnamon
pinch ground ginger
1 tbs (½ tbs) (½ tbs) aniseed
3-4 drops aniseed oil
1 tbs (½ tbs) (½ tbs) ginger syrup
salt

1. Grind the hazelnuts in a pestle and mortar or in a food processor.
2. Beat the butter with the sugar until it is light and creamy.
3. Add the eggs one by one and beat well.
4. Sift the flour with the cinnamon and ginger and work this into the creamed butter mixture.
5. Add the aniseed, aniseed oil, ginger syrup and a little salt to taste. Finally, stir in the ground hazelnuts and knead lightly to make a soft dough.
6. Wrap the dough in plastic film and chill for 1 hour in the refrigerator.
7. Roll out the dough to a large rectangular shape about 1 cm (½ inch) thick and cut it into strips 2 x 4 cm (1 x 2 inches).
8. Place the pastry strips on a lightly greased baking sheet and bake for approximately 10 minutes in a preheated oven (170 °C) (350 °F) or until they are light golden brown in colour.
9. Remove the biscuits from the oven and make a small indentation with your thumb in the top of each one. Leave to cool on a wire tray and store in an airtight biscuit tin.

Note:
These delicious cookies are a speciality from the northern Dutch province of Friesland, they are known as 'Fryske dumkes' (Frisian thumbs). Omit the aniseed oil if this is not available in your area, but a good chemist or health food shop should have supplies.

Apricot flan

(Limburgse vlaai)

500 g (1 lb) (4 cups) flour
salt
approx. 1½ dl (5 fl oz) (2/3 cup) milk
20 g (¾ oz) (¾ ounce) fresh yeast
1 large egg
100 g (4 oz) (½ cup) melted butter
100 g (4 oz) (2/3 cup) caster sugar
approx. 900 g (2 lb) (2 pounds) apricot compote
16 apricot halves, fresh or tinned

1. Sift the flour with a pinch of salt in a large mixing bowl. Warm the milk and cream the yeast with the milk, in a small bowl. Leave in a warm place until it starts to froth.
2. Make a hollow in the mound of flour and pour in the creamed yeast. Stir the yeast mixture into the flour.
3. Add the beaten egg, melted butter and sugar and knead to a soft dough which easily comes away from the sides of the bowl.
4. Shape the dough into a ball, cover the basin with a damp cloth and leave for about 1 hour in a warm place until the dough is well risen. Preheat the oven to 230 °C (450 °F).
5. Lightly grease two large flat flan tins. Knead the risen dough on a lightly floured work surface and use it to line the flan tins. Cover the dough with apricot compote and garnish with halved apricots. Bake for 15-25 minutes in the centre of the oven.
6. Cool the flans on a wire tray and serve with whipped cream.

Tip:
Apricots are in abundance during the summer months – fresh ones are far tastier than the tinned variety. Left over compote can be served as a vegetable with fried or baked sausages or pork chops and fried potatoes.

Variation:
This special fruit flan from the southern Dutch province of Limburg can also be decorated with a trellis work of pastry. Use slightly less dough for the base of the flan and cover the fruit compote

with a trellis work of pastry strips, approximately 1 cm (½ inch) wide.
Use apple or cherry compote as a filling, instead of the apricots and if fresh fruit is not available, use a commercial fruit pie filling.

Frisian cookies

(Drabbelkoeken)

makes approx. 1½ kg (3 lb) (3 pounds)

A speciality from the northern Dutch province of Friesland. These biscuits resemble waffles and are fried in butter instead of baked in the oven. The specially shaped funnel (with three tubes) can be purchased in well stocked hardware stores, especially in Friesland itself.

350 g (12 oz) (3 cups) flour
225 g (8 oz) (2 cups) buckwheat flour
350 g (12 oz) (1¾ cups) sugar
1 tsp (½ tsp) (½ tsp) ground cinnamon
pinch salt
3 medium eggs
5 dl (17 fl oz) (2 cups) milk
300 g (10 oz) (1¼ cups) butter

1. Sift the flour, buckwheat flour, sugar, ground cinnamon and a pinch of salt to taste in a large bowl and mix well.
2. Lightly beat the eggs in a small basin with a spoonful of milk and stir this into the sifted flour. Gradually add the remaining milk to make a smooth, thick batter.
3. Melt the butter in a large heavy based frying pan, but do not allow it to brown.
4. Ladle a little of the batter into the special funnel and allow the batter to fall into the melted butter, turning the funnel with a circular movement at the same time. Instead of using the funnel you can simple spoon small mounds of batter into the pan and fry them in the same way.
5. Fry the cookies gently until they are golden brown on both sides and drain on crumpled kitchen paper.
6. Store in an airtight tin in a cool place, but eat them within 2 weeks of making them, otherwise the butter may become rancid.

Poffertjes
Visitors to Holland may treat themselves to a portion of 'poffertjes' at one of the many street cafes. These are small pancake puffs fried on a special hotplate with small indentations. The 'poffertjes' frier is very skilled at his job and it is well worth taking a little time to watch him flipping over the crispy, golden puffs of pancake batter. The 'poffertjes' are then dusted liberally with icing sugar and served piping hot. Small 'poffertjes' pans are also available at most hardware stores in Holland – here is a recipe for those who may have purchased one as a souvenir. Recipe on page 95.

The feast of Saint Nicolas

(Sinterklaas)

As far as Dutch children are concerned the 5th of December is far more important than the 25th of December. This is the day that Saint Nicolas, the patron saint of children, visits every Dutch home with gifts for all, but especially for the children. Preparations begin some 10 days before hand. Sinterklaas (St. Nicolas) arrives by boat from Spain, accompanied by his Moorish servant Black Peter (Zwarte Piet), attired in 17th century Spanish costume. Almost every evening Dutch children fill one of their shoes with hay, bread or a carrot for Sinterklaas' horse and sing special songs before going to bed. Next morning, the food has been replaced by a small present, usually a chocolate letter (the child's initial) or a marzipan sweet. Larger presents are exchanged on the evening of the 5th December. The presents are delivered in a large sack at the front door and they all contain a short rhyme pertaining to the character of the person concerned which has to be read aloud. As with most special occasions it is traditional to eat and drink certain things. Here are a few recipes for particular specialities which are served up at this festive time of the year.

Marzipan

(Marsepein)

See photo on page 111.

500 g (1 lb) (4 cups) blanched almonds or 500 g
(1 lb) (5 cups) ground almonds
1 kg (2 lb) (2 pounds) icing sugar
3 egg whites
2-3 tsp (1½ – 2 tsp) (1½ – 2 tsp) rose water

1. Grind whole almonds in a pestle and mortar or in a food processor and mix with the sugar.
2. Lightly beat the egg whites and stir them into the ground almonds and sugar, together with the rose water. Knead to a soft dough.
3. Wrap the marzipan in plastic film and chill in the refrigerator.

4. Colour small pieces of marzipan with natural food colourings and shape them into fruit or animals, or simply coat small balls of marzipan with a little cocoa or drinking chocolate powder.

Tip:
Wrap any unused marzipan in plastic film and store in the refrigerator.

Hard fondant

(Roomborstplaat)

1 orange, ½ grapefruit or 1 large lemon
approx. 4 sugar lumps
5 tbs (4 tbs) (4 tbs) cream or lightly soured cream
200 g (7 oz) (1 cup) sugar
½ tbs (1 tsp) (1 tsp) butter

1. Scrub the fruit with a clean brush and rub the skin with the sugar lumps.
2. Pour the cream into a heavy based pan and add the sugar lumps and sugar.
3. Bring the cream slowly to the boil, stirring all the time and cook gently until the mixture is thick and syrupy. It should fall from a spoon in a thin thread.
4. Remove the pan from the heat, stir in the butter and continue stirring until the mixture becomes opaque.
5. Spoon it quickly into small lightly greased patty tins or small lightly greased metal biscuit cutters, placed on a sheet of greased aluminium foil. Leave until hard. Turn out and wrap in coloured cellophane paper if wished.

Chocolate fondant

(Chocolade borstplaat)

200 g (7 oz) (1 cup) sugar
5 tbs (4 tbs) (4 tbs) cream
1 tbs (½ tbs) (½ tbs) cocoa powder
½ tbs (1 tsp) (1 tsp) butter

Prepare the fondant with the sugar, cream and cocoa powder as described in the previous recipe for hard fondant.

Spiced cookies

(Speculaas)

See photo on previous page

makes approx. 900 g (2 lb) (2 pounds) spiced
cookies

*400 g (14 oz) (3½ cups) self raising flour or plain
flour with 1 tsp baking powder*
200 g (7 oz) (1½ cups) soft brown sugar
pinch salt
approx. 75 g (3 oz) (1 cup) cake crumbs
150 g (6 oz)(¾ cup) butter
3 tbs (2 tbs) (2 tbs) mixed spice
a little finely grated lemon peel
5 tbs (4 tbs) (4 tbs) milk
flour

1. Sift the flour with the sugar and a pinch of salt
into a large bowl. Stir in the cake crumbs, the butter, cut into small pieces, the mixed spice and a
little grated lemon peel to taste. Rub the butter into
the other ingredients until the mixture resembles
fine breadcrumbs, add the milk, a little at a time,
and knead quickly and lightly to a soft dough.
2. Preheat the oven to 170 °C (350 °F) and lightly
grease a baking sheet. Dust a wooden shortbread
mould with a little flour. (Special 'speculaas'
moulds are available in Holland, but a wooden
shortbread mould will do just as well.) Press the
dough into the mould and trim the edges.
3. Invert the mould onto the baking sheet and tap
gently to remove the dough in one piece. Clean the
mould with kitchen paper, dust it with flour and repeat the process until all the dough has been used.
4. Bake the cookies for approximately 25 minutes
in the centre of the oven until they are golden
brown. Cool for a few minutes on the baking sheet
and then slide them onto a wire tray and leave until
completely cold.

Tip:
These spiced cookies can also be decorated with
flaked or whole almonds. Press them carefully into
the shaped dough, just before baking.
This recipe can also be used to make conventional
cookies. Roll out the dough and shape into cookies
with a plain or fluted cutter. Bake for about 15 minutes and cool on a wire tray.

Christmas rings

(Kerstkransjes)

makes approx. 1 kg (2 lb) (2 pounds) cookies

200 g (7 oz) (1⅓ cups) caster sugar
8 g (2 tsp) (2 tsp) vanilla sugar
400 g (14 oz) (3½ cups) flour
300 g (12 oz) (1¼ cups) butter
2 lightly beaten eggs
pinch salt
milk or 1 egg yolk
40 g (1½ oz) (2 tbs) sugar
50 g (2 oz) (½ cup) flaked almonds

1. Sift the caster sugar, vanilla sugar and flour into
a large mixing bowl. Cut the butter into small pieces and rub them into the flour until the mixture resembles fine breadcrumbs.
2. Add the beaten eggs and a pinch of salt and
knead quickly and lightly to make a soft dough.
Dust the work surface with flour and roll out the
pastry to a thickness of ½ cm (¼ inch).
3. Stamp out small cookies, using a fluted cutter
and then cut a small circle of dough out of the centre of each with an applecorer. Preheat the oven to
approximately 160 °C (325 °F).
4. Brush the cookies with a little milk or lightly
beaten egg yolk and sprinkle them with sugar and
flaked almonds.
5. Lift them onto a lightly greased baking sheet and
bake for about 25 minutes in the centre of the oven.
Cool on a wire tray and store in an airtight tin.

Savoury thins

(Zoute stengels)

See photo on page 114-115.

makes approx. 500 g (1 lb) (1 pound)

250 g (8 oz) (1 cup) cold butter
15 g (1 tbs) (1 tbs) salt
250 g (8 oz) (2 cups) flour
1 small lightly beaten egg

1. Cut the butter into small pieces and put them into a large mixing bowl, together with the salt and the flour. Cut the butter into the flour, using 2 knives instead of rubbing it in with the hands – it is important that the mixture remains as cool as possible – and knead to a crumbly dough.
2. Sprinkle the work surface with flour and roll the pastry out to a thickness of 3 mm (⅛ inch). Add a little extra flour if the pastry becomes sticky.
3. Fold the dough into three and roll it out once more. Repeat this rolling and folding twice more, fold the dough, wrap it in plastic film and chill in the refrigerator for 15-20 minutes.
4. Repeat the whole rolling and folding procedure twice more, not forgetting to chill the pastry in between.
5. Roll the pastry out to a large square – preheat the oven to 220 °C (425 °F).
6. Lightly grease a large baking sheet and sprinkle it with a little salt. Lift the pastry onto the sheet and cut it into strips approximately 8 x 1½ cm (5 x ½ inch). Brush them with lightly beaten egg and bake for about 10 minutes at the top of the oven, reduce the heat to 160 °C (325 °F) and bake for a further 20-25 minutes or until they are golden brown and well crisped.

Variation:
Replace half of the butter with 125 g (5 oz) (1½ cups) grated semi-mature (Dutch) cheese. Sprinkle the cheese over the dough during the rolling and folding procedure and complete the recipe as above.

Salted cocktail snacks

(Zoute bollen)

See photo on page 114-115.

makes approx. 400 g (14 oz) (14 ounces) cocktail snacks

15 g (½ oz) (½ ounce) fresh yeast or 7 g (¼ oz)
(2 tsp) dried yeast
approx. 1 dl (3½ fl oz) (½ cup) lukewarm milk
300 g (10 oz) (2½ cups) flour
15 g (½ oz) (1 tbs) salt
1 lightly beaten egg
20-40 g (1-2 oz) (2-4 tbs) melted butter

1. Cream the yeast with a little of the warm milk and leave in a warm place until it starts to froth.
2. Sift the flour and salt into a large bowl. Make a hollow in the top of the flour, pour in the creamed yeast, the rest of the warm milk, the lightly beaten egg and melted butter and knead to a smooth dough.
3. Place the dough in the basin, cover with a damp cloth and leave in a warm place for about 1 hour, or until the dough is well risen.
4. Shape small pieces of the risen dough into marble sized balls, place them on lightly greased baking sheets and cover with damp cloths. Leave in a warm place for about 15 minutes and preheat the oven to 200 °C (400 °F)
5. Bake the cocktail snacks for about 12 minutes in the centre of the oven, or until they are well risen and golden brown.
6. Open the oven door, reduce the heat to 120 °C (250 °F) and bake for a further 30 minutes or until the snacks are crisp.

Variation:
Knead 2 tablespoons of finely chopped stem ginger into the dough, roll it out and cut out small shapes with a cooky cutter. Bake as described above.

On the following page a selection of home made and purchased savoury cocktail snacks.

Brandied raisins

(Boerenjongens)

See photo on page 117.

500 g (1 lb) (3 cups) yellow raisins or sultanas
approx. 200 g (7 oz) (1⅓ cups) caster sugar
½ cinnamon stick
approx. 8 dl (1⅓ pts) (3½ cups) Dutch brandy
(brandewijn) or preserving alcohol

1. Wash the raisins and drain in a sieve.
2. Bring approximately 2½ dl (8 fl oz) (1 cup) water to the boil in a heavy based pan and sprinkle in the sugar. Add the cinnamon stick and stir over a gentle heat until the sugar has completely dissolved.
3. Stir in the raisins and simmer them very gently for about 30 minutes in the warm syrup. Cool, cover the pan and refrigerate overnight.
4. Spoon the raisins and sugar syrup into a sterilised preserving jar, pour in the brandy and seal the bottle.
5. Keep for at least 7-8 weeks in a cool, dark place before serving.

Tip:
Nut enthusiasts can add a few blanched almonds or hazelnuts along with the brandy.

Note:
In Holland 'Boerenjongens' are served in a small glass and eaten with a tiny silver spoon. It is important to use clear preserving alcohol which is 48% proof.

Brandied apricots

(Boerenmeisjes)

See photo on page 117.

300 g (10 oz) (10 ounces) dried apricots
approx. 250 g (8 oz) (1½ cups) caster sugar
small piece of lemon peel
approx. 8 dl (1⅓ pts) (3½ cups) Dutch brandy
(brandewijn) or preserving alcohol

1. Wash the apricots and drain in a sieve.
2. Bring 3 dl (½ pt) (1¼ cups) water to the boil in a heavy based pan and sprinkle in the sugar. Stir over a gentle heat until the sugar has dissolved completely.
3. Add the apricots and the lemon peel, bring to the boil and simmer gently for about 10 minutes.
4. Cool and refrigerate overnight in the covered pan.
5. Spoon the fruit and syrup into a sterilised preserving jar and add the brandy. Seal and keep for at least 7-8 weeks in a cool, dark place before serving.

Tip:
Brandied sultanas or apricots can also be served with vanilla ice cream or in a coupe dish with plenty of unsweetened lightly whipped cream.

Bishop's wine

(Bisschopswijn)

7 dl (1¼ pts) (3 cups) red wine
1 orange or 2 mandarin oranges
4 cloves
small piece cinnamon stick
1 whole nutmeg
60 g (2 oz) (⅓ cup) caster sugar

1. Heat the wine gently with approximately 7 dl (1¼ pts) (3 cups) water in a large heavy based pan.
2. Stud the well scrubbed orange with the cloves and infuse it in the wine for about an hour, together with the cinnamon and the nutmeg. The wine must not be allowed to come to the boil.
3. Strain the Bishop's wine into a clean jug and add sugar to taste.
4. Serve in wine glasses.

Left: brandied apricots. Right: brandied raisins.

Farmer's beer

(Warme ketel)

4 dl (14 fl oz) (1¾ cups) Dutch brandy (brandewijn)
4 bottles brown ale
approx. 100 g (4 oz) (¾ cup) soft brown sugar

1. Pour the brandy and beer into a heavy based pan, sprinkle in the sugar and bring the contents of the pan slowly to the boil.
2. Remove the pan from the heat just as the liquid reaches boiling point.
3. Pour into stone beer mugs and serve with sliced pumpernickle and thinly sliced smoked boiled bacon.

Note:
This recipe comes from the Frisian island of Terschelling and was traditionally drunk when tenant farmers came to pay their rent to the landlord.

Berry brandy

(Cassia)

2 kg (4 lb) (8 cups) sugar
2 l (3¼ pts) (8 cups) Dutch brandy (brandewijn)
800 g (1½ lb) (1½ pounds) raspberries
800 g (1½ lb) (1½ pounds) red or black currants

1. Sterilize a large preserving jar with boiling soda water and drain upside down on a clean teatowel.
2. Dissolve the sugar in about 5 dl (17 fl oz) (2 cups) boiling water in a heavy based pan and stir over a gentle heat until it forms a thin syrup.
3. Add the brandy and stir well.
4. Clean the raspberries and the red or black currants and stir them into the brandy and sugar syrup.
5. Shake the jar, cover and infuse for 7-8 days in a cool dark place, shaking the jar carefully every day.
6. Strain the contents through a piece of butter muslin and pour into clean preserving jars.
7. Seal the jars and store for at least 3 months in a cool, dry place. Strain once more through a clean piece of muslin and pour into clean jars.

Note:
Cassia is traditionally drunk at weddings in the province of Gelderland, East Holland. Any leftover cassia should be kept in the refrigerator and served slightly chilled.

Aniseed brandy

(Steernties or Steranijs)

approx. 450 g (1 lb) (1 pound) white candy sugar
small piece of saffron or approx. ½ tsp (¼ tsp) (¼ tsp) ground saffron
approx. 15 g (½ oz) (1 tbs) star aniseed
7 dl (1¼ pts) (3 cups) Dutch brandy (brandewijn)

1. Sterilize a preserving jar with boiling soda water and drain upside down on a clean teatowel.
2. Put the candy sugar, saffron and star aniseed into the jar.
3. Pour in the brandy, seal the bottle and shake well.
4. Store the aniseed brandy for 7-8 weeks, shaking the jar occasionally until the candy sugar has dissolved.
5. Strain the mixture through a clean piece of butter muslin and pour into a clean preserving jar. Seal the jar.
6. Serve the aniseed brandy with ice cubes or mineral water.

Note:
Star aniseed was originally a Chinese spice and tastes a quite different to ordinary aniseed. Today, it is often ground and combined with other spices to make the famous 5-spice powder, so often used in Chinese cookery. It may be interesting for gardening enthusiasts to know that it is the fruit of the star aniseed tree (Hicium verum Hooker).
Star aniseed used to be prescribed by herbalists as a tranquiliser, today it is more often found in the kitchen. Both seeds and pods can be used, but only in small amounts as they tend to mask other flavours.

Egg nog with cinnamon

(Kandeel)

See photo on page 120-121.

1 stick cinnamon
5 cloves
the peel of 1 lemon
8-10 egg yolks
150 g (6 oz) (¾ cup) caster sugar
7 dl (1¼ pt) (3 cups) semisweet wine

1. Infuse the cinnamon, cloves and lemon peel for about 1 hour in a little hot water and then strain before use.
2. Lightly beat the egg yolks with the sugar until they are light and creamy and then gradually beat in the wine.
3. Stir in the spice infusion and pour into the top half of a bain-marie, or into a bowl placed over a pan of hot water. Heat gently, stirring occasionally, until the mixture has thickened slightly.
4. Serve in warm cups or heatproof glasses.

Note:
Kandeel has been served in Holland for centuries to women recovering from childbirth.

Advocaat

(Advocaat)

1 vanilla pod
12 eggs
approx. 350 g (12 oz) (1¾ cups) sugar
7 dl (1¼ pts) (3 cups) Dutch brandy (brandewijn)

1. Split the vanilla pod and scrape out the soft centre. Whisk the eggs, sugar and scraped out vanilla in a warm, enamel bowl until the mixture becomes thick and pale and leaves a trail when dropped from the beaters.
2. Gradually beat in the brandy and continue beating until the eggs and brandy are well mixed.
3. Set the bowl over a pan of hot water and stir until the advocaat is smooth and thick. Regulate the heat so that the water in the pan stays just below boiling point.
4. Leave the advocaat to cool, stirring occasionally to prevent a skin from forming and store in sterilised bottles with tight fitting lids.

Tip:
Advocaat can be stored for up to 2 months in a cool dark place.
Use as a filling for cakes and gateaux or as a garnish for custards and sweet mousses.

Note:
Advocaat garnished with a rosette of whipped cream is a favourite drink amongst women in Holland and although it is classified as a drink it is actually eaten with a small spoon.

On the following pages: Egg nog with cinnamon – traditionally served when visiting a new born baby.

Hot chocolate

(Chocolademelk)

1 l (1¾ pts) (4 cups) milk
50 g (2 oz) (⅓ cup) cocoa
50 g (2 oz) (¼ cup) sugar

1. Bring the milk slowly to the boil.
2. Mix the cocoa and the sugar in a small basin and blend in a few spoonfuls of the warm milk.
3. Return the blend to the milk in the pan, whisk well and then simmer gently for about 4 minutes.
4. Pour the hot chocolate into beakers or heatproof glasses and serve immediately.

Spiced milk

(Slemp)

1 l (1¾ pts) (4 cups) milk
½ cinnamon stick
small piece of saffron or ½ tsp (¼ tsp) (¼ tsp)
ground saffron, 3 cloves
small piece of mace
½ tsp (¼ tsp) (¼ tsp) tea
40 g (1½ oz) (3 tbs) sugar
2 tsp (1 tsp) (1 tsp) cornflour, cornstarch or rice flour

1. Bring the milk to the boil in a heavy based pan and add the cinnamon, saffron, cloves, mace and tea. Simmer very gently for about 45 minutes, strain and sweeten with the sugar.
2. Blend the cornflour with a spoonful of cold water and then use it to thicken the spiced milk.
3. Serve piping hot. The amount of spices used may need to be adjusted according to taste. The flavour of the tea and mace should not mask the flavour of the saffron and cinnamon.

Note:
A hot beverage with a historic background. Spiced milk was a popular drink long before tea and coffee were introduced into Europe. The tea in this recipe is quite a recent addition. In Holland it is still drunk in certain provinces.

Aniseed milk

(Anijsmelk)

1 l (1¾ pts) (4 cups) milk
1½ tbs (1 tbs) (1 tbs) aniseed
50 g (2 oz) (¼ cup) sugar
1½ tbs (1 tbs) (1 tbs) cornflour or cornstarch

1. Bring the milk to the boil in a heavy based pan.
2. Tie the aniseed in a small piece of butter muslin and infuse this for about 25 minutes in the hot milk. Remove and discard the aniseed. Strain the milk and return to the heat.
3. Add the sugar and stir until it has dissolved.
4. Blend the cornflour with 2 spoonfuls of cold water and use this to thicken the milk.
5. Pour the milk into small cups or bowls and serve with the Frisian hazelnut cookies described on page 108.

Tip:
Aniseed cubes can also be used instead of aniseed. Allow 6-7 cubes to 1 l (1¾ pts) (4 cups) milk and add them together with the sugar.
The cornflour can be omitted if preferred.

Iced tea

(IJsthee)

1 l (1¾ pts) (4 cups) water
3 teabags
75 g (3 oz) (⅓ cup) sugar
the juice of 1 lemon
1 lemon

1. Bring the water to the boil in a large pan, remove from the heat and infuse the teabags for about 4 minutes.
2. Discard the teabags, dissolve the sugar in the hot tea and add the lemon juice.
3. Allow to cool completely and then chill for about 3 hours in the refrigerator.
4. Pour the tea into tall glasses, add to each glass a few ice cubes and garnish the rim of each glass with a slice of lemon.

Index

Index

Index